ASA

HONORING HIS LIFE AND WORK

Edited by Dr. James Young & Dr. Itihari Toure

Chicago, Illinois

Front cover illustration by Damon Stanford

Copyright © 2013 by James Young & Itihari Toure

First Edition, First Printing

Printed in the United States of America

ISBN #: 1-934155-84-5

ISBN #: 978-1934-155-844

Contents

Preface

The **Collective** efforts of the editors represents more than 100 years of professional service in the field of teacher education, community involvement and community participation. Their combined teaching experiences cut across preschool, elementary, middle, high school, and higher education. Included in their professional endeavors were independent and public school experiences.

Each had a very special relationship with Dr. Asa G. Hilliard. The combined years of knowing and working directly with Asa exceeded 100 years. We used our best efforts in preparing this set of essays. Asa was widely known and his footprints went beyond the bounds of education. The seven writers who contributed to the work honoring Asa represent early childhood, middle, high school education, Black Women's Studies, psychology, federal policies impacting children and families, assessment, evaluation and research, and theology.

We wanted to address a variety of topics we thought were befitting to the work of Dr. Hilliard. Our goal was to pull together a "representative" selection of critical issues facing the survival of the African community throughout the Diaspora. The writers whose essays are collected in this book are, if not household names, important brothers and sisters in their individual fields. Without exception, they personify what it "means" to be a Jegna.

WE would be negligent if we did not acknowledge the wholesome relationship between Dr. Asa G. Hilliard and Dr. John Henrik Clarke. They stood in tandem on the significance of Africa. They understood the importance of the African family from a historical perspective. Dr. Clarke often reminded us of the greatest achievement of the first African family, at a different time is no less than the greatest achievement of the African family today – our continued survival.

We would hope that readers of these essays would respect our honoring the work of Dr. Hilliard and use the paradigm as outlined in the Introduction by Dr. Toure in that context. To honor Asa is to understand what he stood for as a warrior.

Editors: James C. Young and Itihari Toure

Asa's Bio

Asa Grant Hilliard, III, Ed.D., a.k.a. Nana Baffour Amankwatia, II was a giant of a man. Dr. Hilliard was born in Galveston, Texas, August 22, 1933. He attended Manual High school, Denver, Colorado, where he was a young scholar and active in extracurricular activities. After graduation, he enrolled at the University of Denver and earned a degree in psychology. He taught mathematics and history in the Denver Public Schools before joining the United States Army, where he served as a 1st Lieutenant, platoon leader and a battalion executive officer in the Third Armored Infantry.

Dr. Hilliard was the third generation of educators. His grandfather and father were outstanding educators and principals. He was a diligent servant of humanity. Asa was described as a Jegna, giant, master teacher, leader, elder, king, chief, good man, genius, humble, powerful thinker, and a wonderful person. He described himself as a teacher, historian, and a psychologist. He was committed to the healthy socialization of African people. Dr. Hilliard was a world renowned Pan-Africanist educator.

Dr. Hilliard served as the Fuller E. Calloway Professor of Urban Education at Georgia State University in Atlanta for twenty-seven years. He held joint appointments in the Department of educational Policy Studies, the Department of Educational Psychology and Special Education. Prior to his tenure at Georgia State University, he served as a consultant to the Peace Corp in Liberia, West Africa as well as the superintendent of school in Monrovia, Liberia. When he returned to his professorship at San Francisco State University, he served as department chair, and later, as Dean of Education. His tenure in those positions is legendary.

Dr. Hilliard was an esteemed expert. He was a Board Certified Forensic Examiner and Diplomat of both the American Board of Forensic Examiners and the American Board of Forensic Medicine. He served as a lead expert witness in several landmark federal cases on test validity and bias, including Larry P. v. Wilson Riles in California, Mattie T. v. Mississippi, Deborah P. v. Turlington in Florida, and also two Supreme Court cases, Ayers v. Fordice in Mississippi, and Marino v. Ortiz in New York City.

Dr. Hilliard lived a life based on the principle of excellence in study, preparation and research. He authored more than several hundred publications, including journal articles, magazine articles, special reports, chapters in books, and books. Some of his publications include The Maroon Within Us: Selected Essays on African American Community Socialization (Black Classic Press, 1995); The Reawakening of the African Mind (Makare Publishing, 1997); African Power: Affirming African Indigenous Socialization in the Face of the Cultural Wars (Makare Publishing, 2002). He co-edited the Teachings of Ptahhotep, the Oldest Book in the World, with Larry Williams, and Nia Damali, (Blackwood Press, 1987) and Young, Gifted, and Black: Promoting High Achievement Among African American Students (Beacon Press, 2004).

Dr. Hilliard's research reached thousands through his video and television productions, including Self Determination and Free Your Mind, Return to the Source. He led numerous study tours to Egypt and Ghana, for more than thirty years. This was part of his mission of teaching the truth about the history of Africa and the African Diaspora. The ancestral ties to Africa were more than intellectual ones for him. He considered teaching a sacred task. In 2001, Dr. Hilliard was enstooled as Development Chief for Mankranso, Ghana, and given the name Nana Baffour Amankwatia II, which means "generous one."

As a result of his unselfishness, his footprints for service were imprinted in various organizations. He was a former board member of the American association for Colleges of Teacher Education, a founding member of the National Black Child Development Institute, a founding member of the Association for the Study of Classical African Civilization and was a key advisor for the African Education for Every Child Conference held in Mali.

Family was very important to Dr. Hilliard. He was married to Pasty Jo Hilliard for nearly 50 years. They had four children, and a host of grandchildren.

We are because you are.

Chapter 1: Framing the Discourse (Achieving Educational Excellence for African People: History, Philosophy, Theory & Pragmatics)

By Itihari Toure

The Asafication[1] of educational excellence is a signal that some Africans take seriously our responsibility for inter-generational social transmission, for raising our own children, and for continuing to raise us. We acknowledge the ancient African foundations of deep thought and deep spirituality from which our excellent practices sprang, and from which further development is possible. In doing this, we join the process of Sankofa, reaching back to the African ideals of MAAT, deny-ing the authority and legitimacy of the Maafa, the great terror of slavery, colonization, segregation/apartheid, and the ide-ology of white supremacy, and any other form of domination over us. We look forward to constructing our own future, from our past, so that we may, in the words of Kimbwandende Kia Bunseki Fu-Kiau, "stand on our own ground."

So many of our people are marching toward their own termination, even begging to be led by aliens, who have shown in every way that they do not have our interests at heart. Many of us have become alien to ourselves, even anti-self, as Naim Akbar has shown. We have great amnesia regarding our past, we have become dependent and disoriented, and therefore, we have become a danger and a threat as teachers of our young. We have come to know our own children through the views and language of our oppressors, feeling quite comfortable liv-ing up to the standards of others (Hilliard, 2004). The topics and commentaries in this first installment on 'doing Asa" series attest to this reality.

The disregard of cultural and social memory, the dependence upon others to define who, how and when we are is a critical aspect of education for social transmission. How one locates oneself defines our being. When we locate African people in the context of failure and dysfunction then our being is one of failure and dysfunction. We produce failure and dysfunction. We do not and we will not exist. When we locate African people in the context of our cultural excellence, we produce excellence and we build for eternity. The framing for this collection (doing Asa) reflects this understanding in his statement "To Be Afrikan Or Not Be" (Hilliard, 2000):

Cultural Memory	**Our Being/Doing**	**Results**	**Eternity**
Absence/Disregard or African Cultural Memory ⟷	Fearful Dysfunctional Powerless ⟷	Failure ⟶	Nonexistence

Cultural Memory	**Our Being/Doing**	**Results**	**Eternity**
Present/Regard For African Worldview ⟷	Powerful Courageous ⟷ Effective	Excellence ⟶	Building For Eternity

To change this trajectory of collective destruction is not difficult as some would have us to believe. It does require a different point of trajectory about *Who* we are, *How* we are, and *When* we are African. Our understanding and engagement of location begins with recalling our African worldview and the function of deep thought, as observed in this book; for example, in Chike Akua's "Education and Culture in Context" and Reverend Dr. Mark Lomax's "Spirituality and Leadership in the Afrikan Church in North America." When we discern our African worldview, deep thought and mastery in the context of what we do and how we are in the world, we also discover specific characteristics of those who are equipped to produce excellence. Read, for example, Dr. Charlyn Harper Browne's "On Preparing 'Ready Early Childhood Educators'" and Drs. Ernest Washington and James Young's "Gaining Credibility and Losing 'Knowledge,' 'We,' and Cultural Validity." These persons, organizations, and communities are courageous; they uphold the truth and protect African culture and African people; they are tested in battle for the liberation and wholeness of African people; and they produce an exceptionally high quality of work that walks the walk of cultural mastery and scholarship. These persons, organizations, and communities speak the success of doing Asa. (See also "The Jegna as a Community of Excellence.")

The process of being Afrikan in the context of white supremacy, cultural hegemony, and oppression requires a specific understanding, analysis, and strategic tools to change the trajectory that has been heading us toward the nonexistence of African people. In this book some of our best scholars guide our discussion on these understandings, analyses, and tools to be African. *Honoring Asa: Framing the Discourse* provides points of engagement, critical thinking, and inquiry into the topics and points raised by our scholars. The contributors were selected based on their own work with *SBA: Reawakening the Afrikan Mind* (Hilliard, Makare Publishing, 1997). SBA is a paradigm based on the re-socialization process of infusion, mastery and dissemination of African-centered education espoused and modeled by Baba Asa G. Hilliard III Nana Baffour Amankwatia II (1933-2007).

African-centered education is a transformative learning process that constructs a path to knowledge, understanding and eventual wisdom. There are several significant factors involved in an African education, as noted in the following chapters found in *Honoring Asa*:

- The Infusion of African Culture and Thought ("The Jegna as a Community of Excellence," "Education and Culture in Context," and "Spirituality and Leadership in the Afrikan Church in North America")
- The Act of Power Teaching through Cultural Ethos ("Are We Asking the Right Question? Reflections on Asa Hilliard and the Notion of Objectivity," "Gaining Credibility and Losing 'Knowledge,' 'We,' and Cultural Validity," and "On Preparing 'Ready Early Childhood Educators'")
- The Intergenerational Socialization of This Afrikan Way of Being ("Early Socialization and Education") Afrikan education is both responsive and creative. It is the only response to the state of mis-education and under-education that prevails in our local and global communities (*The State of African Education*, Hilliard, 2000).[1] It is also the creative genius of Afrikan people when we operate out of our cultural and social worldview (Hilliard, 2002).[2] Evidence of this education is in the stories and the experience of those who have taken seriously the path to restore *MAAT*. African education is a spiritual task that produces a type of excellence that connects personal mastery with collective benefit, as illustrated below.

CHAPTER 1: FRAMING THE DISCOURSE
by Dr. Itihari Toure

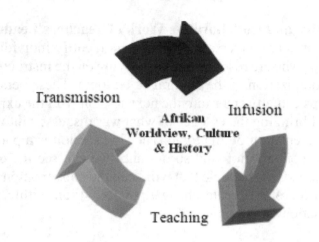

So, what does this reawakening, this "doing Asa" look like in terms of a reciprocal teaching-learning process whether located in the family house, school house, church house or community house? To do Asa is to embody the cultural precepts articulated in *Nsaka Sunsum*—to touch the spirit (Nobles, 2004).[1]

The Synergy in the Flow

The flow of information in this context is circular rather than linear. The decision of what is shared is based on the interrelatedness of the topic and its ability to link with the intent of infusion, teaching and/or transmission. Themes or topics under consideration would be multidimensional in that the theme of topic can be a form of cultural infusion, or pedagogy or socialization. For example, the topic of hip-hop as Afrikan education could be discussed from its content's relevance in Afrikan culture and Afrikan spirituality to its use of Afrikan ways of learning (call-and-response, use of rhythmic interpretation, etc.), to its ability to pass on these very ideas and ways in- and outside of institutional structures.

Collective and Collaborative Work of Teachers/Leaders
In this circular conversation, presenters identify individuals or groups who are responsible for carrying on the instruction/operationalization of the cultural value/topic. These persons or groups actually enter into the next session with the expectation of bringing the essence of what was discussed into the next conversation on the topic. The first session is a part of the next conversation and so on, until we can see the continual threads of the topic that will keep the conversation going and therefore create change/transformation within this conversation on the topic.

The Spirit of Egalitarianism
Those listening in on the conversation are also contributors to the conversation. It is the responsibility of the audience to assist in identifying salient points to be carried into the next level of conversation. What is possible from the audience is the creative crafting of "content relevance" based on the specific settings in which they intend to take the information onward. Imagine a room of students who have different majors or interests; some will be asking: What do I take into the Rites of Passage program I am working with? Others will ask: How will I incorporate this into my academic major and career objectives? The objective of every level is the operationalization of the information for the purpose of either integrating (infusing) it into some other reality, deciding how to operationalize/teach it in an existing setting, or creating some routine/ritual/expression that represents the salient aspects being presented. With this spirit of egalitarianism combined with contributors' active engagement and awareness of practical realities attuned to inquiry and critical thinking, we transform teaching and learning. We contribute tranformatively to an African-centered way of education and socialization.

CHAPTER 1: FRAMING THE DISCOURSE
by Dr. Itihari Toure

Links to Our Transformation and Our Authentic Humanity

There are those of us who are not in a position to guide the teaching or lead the community, yet our presence creates key connections and/or links to those who do guide, lead or teach. Every person in our community potentially makes a contribution to the synergy and spirit of the community. As individuals we are interdependent as is the whole universe. Those who might consider their role inconsequential to this education for African recovery are central to ensuring that the community and the teacher/leader do more than just transmit and receive the information. We all have a role in creating space for the teacher/leader and the community to change/transform from one phase of this process to the next.

Institute Builders

Those involved in institution building are responsible for communicating the intent, logistics and outcome of the institution. An institutional mission to "do Asa"[2] through capturing and practicing a path for African education is a primary outcome. The process of classifying various topics by using the three aspects of African education–who, how, and when we are African—assists teachers/leaders with shaping a lesson, teaching, or analysis and encourages shared investment and shared meaning with those in the institution. This is also an institution-building outcome. Communication from the Institution builders is about more than shaping *what* the Institution is about; it also entails describing *how* the Institution reflects the "Asafication" of our work and our study.

When this contribution to the body of work, legacy and life of Dr. Asa Grant Hilliard III Nana Baffour Amankwatia II is complete, the outcomes will be both personal and collective.

Personally, full understanding of this work produces an outcome that requires one to construct a way of being that produces excellence. This excellence is evidenced by one's ability to establish criteria of high quality and consistent mastery, critical thinking and analysis, and confidence in the inherent genius of African people. Collectively, it provides the consummate example of what is to be whole and what is to be African.

Itihari Toure, EdD
The Jegna Collective
January, 2013

Chapter 2: The Jegna as a Community of Excellence

By Itihari Toure

The Jegna Collective acknowledges the ancient African foundations of deep thought and deep spirituality from which excellent practices sprang, and from which further development is possible. In doing this, the Jegna Collective as a community joins the process of Sankofa, reaching back to the African ideals of *MAAT,* denying the authority and legitimacy of the *Maafa*—the great terrors of slavery, colonization, segregation/apartheid, and the ideology of white supremacy—and any other form of domination over us. Through the purpose and experience of the Jegna Collective we construct an African future from the past, so that African people worldwide in the words of Kimbwandende Kia Bunseki Fu-Kiau can "stand on our own ground" (2003).

Among the many great ancient African teachers, leaders, and healer communities in African traditions and societies is the community in Ethiopia, the Jegnoch. They are fearless, tested in battle, producers of exceptionally high quality of work who commit, at the price of their lives to protect their people, land and culture, and who vow to speak the truth always (Hilliard, 2002). There is no higher model in any culture anywhere than that of the Jegna. In 2002 at the National Black Child Development Institute (NBCDI) Conference Dr. Asa G. Hilliard III, known to some as Nana Baffour Amankwatia II began to describe a way of being that preserved the cultural power evidenced in ancient and contemporary African societies. He shared with those in attendance, the characteristics of a master teacher/healer/warrior revered in the days of ancient Egypt and in contemporary western and northern Africa. Ancient Egypt called them Sebai; in West

Africa, they are Jeli or Jelimuso and in Ethiopia, the personhood of the Jegna would later be institutionalized here in the United States as a model for restoring excellence in African education (Hilliard, 2002).[1] Another living tradition in West Africa is found among the Dogon's eminent levels of education and spiritual development. During the NBCDI conference in 2002, educators, historians, spiritual leaders, and activists in Atlanta, Georgia combined the Dogona concept of "sight" with the Jegna tradition as a basis for recreating a transformational and social transmission process here in the Diaspora Africana.

The Jegna is one response that Dr. Hilliard articulated on the conditions of African education, his foremost endeavor to which we pay tribute in part with *Honoring Asa: Framing the Discourse.* As such, this contribution to the discourse describes the disposition and function of the Jegna as a relevant and effective response to the state of African education. It is important to share the context from which Dr. Hilliard galvanized educators, researchers, students, activists, and spiritual leaders to the way of the Jegna here in Atlanta and wherever he was asked to speak internationally. The personhood of the Jegna not only addresses the challenge of restoring excellence in African education it also responds to one of the most important final areas of work for Dr. Hilliard, renewing a process of social transmission among African people that ensures our survival and our thriving for future generations.

Development of the Jegna Collective as a Community
Initially, the Jegna Collective established a framework which its education and experiences would consistently reflect. The work and education of the Collective is:
- For all Afrikans, not merely for teachers;
- Through age-graded cohorts, it is a life-spanning process;
- Community-controlled, -designed and -led by wise, independent elders;

10

CHAPTER 2: THE JEGNA AS A COMMUNITY OF EXCELLENCE by Dr. Itihari Toure

- Community-centered and -rooted;
- More than schooling—our analyses must not be limited to what goes on in public schools; the framework reflects a team process to produce a Pan-African consciousness and belonging.

The expected outcome of the Jegna Collective is a communal healing through models of excellence in specific categories. The experiences of the Collective bring these examples to mind holistically not episodically, using diverse cultural, communications, social, and educational means. Although the experiences and education are diverse, there is a consistent presentation of holistic approaches through the references and resources about the other categories. In the Jegna Collective introduction to these categories is called "Afrientation":

Community renewal, sustenance, and service

Personal growth and development of character and values

Cultural acquisition and transmission

Knowledge, skills, and wisdom

Health and well-being

Environmental protection and nurture

Spiritual development

Family identity, belonging, bonding

Linkages to families and children

Assumption of responsibilities for self/community

Essentially, these categories generate a charge to recover and restore those models in all aspects of our living. To accomplish this, the Collective strives to stimulate a passion for study and research, scholarship and service that demonstrate those models of excellence wherever they are in our history and in the current realities of African people.

HONORING ASA BY DOING ASA

Education as Sacred
In our tradition, education is a spiritual task. Those involved as educators saw themselves as having a "calling"—whether they acted upon this devotion to education during ancient times in Africa or during more recent eras throughout the Diaspora as they sought teaching and learning experiences. The goal of the educational process is to touch the spirit and discover our spiritual path, which is the reason for our existence. The Jegna Collective seeks the spiritual nature in all aspects of our socialization and strives to rekindle the relationship we have as a people to our spiritual destiny. The experiences of the Jegna Collective are all spiritually driven and spiritually contextualized.

The Creation and Practice of Rituals of the Jegnoch
Part of that spiritual journey involves recovering, creating, and practicing those social traditions and rituals that reinforce Afrikan power in all of its forms. We embrace the worldview of *ubuntu,* originating among the people of southern Africa; *ubuntu* encourages the acknowledgment, value and role of our ancestors in all that we do, in the spirit of resistance, in our struggle to regain our power, and in the preservation and sanctity of our culture.

The mission of the Jegna Collective and its role in the Afrikan community is clear, because it is present and guided by the Ancestors. Its structure, experiences, and processes as a community are developing as we continue to grow and develop; however, it is important to establish key aspects of an infrastructure for those persons who become involved with the Jegna Collective so that the mission is understood. It is also important that we continue to define *the ways in which the Collective acts.* One part of this definition entails how the Jegna Collective functions as a community and sustains a healthy, inclusive, and balanced environment for the re-socialization and instruction of those persons who choose the

sojourn of the Jegnoch. The other part of this definition involves how we work as Conveners, Spirit Guides, Sebai, and
Initiates as we reflect collective leadership that emphasizes
consistent engagement, assumed responsibility, and account-
ability.

Roles within the Jegna Collective

The Conveners assume full responsibility for every aspect of
the Jegna Collective. Therefore, the Conveners directly connect their own journey with our collective memory and recall
ways of being that are in alignment with our Afrikan sense of
communal organization. The work of the Conveners is to contribute significantly in re-invigorating Afrikan standards of
excellence through transformation. The Conveners facilitate
this transformation through creating experiences and opportunities to:

Build communities;

Learn an African language;

Politically educate;

Study victories;

Study economics and economic development for our
community;

Teach students and initiates how to provide cultural
transmission;

Teach the skill and knowledge needed to organize, to
size up strengths and weaknesses;

Learn how to produce community ownership;

Learn to solve real problems.

This results in "Nation Building" and the rescue and recon-
struction of Africa and African-based civilizations.

Personal and Collective Transformation

Personal and Collective Transformation is situated in the role
and relationship of the Council of Jegnoch (elders), Sebai (master
teachers), and initiates. Initiates are educators in development

who chose the Jegna Collective as the community of engagement for their own transformation as Afrikan persons. Our convening and participating engages us in their transformation as they are in us as a community.

Character and behavior are also extremely important aspects of our community. This is visualized and assisted by the Spirit Guides in the presentation and demonstration of values, which speak to the respect of human and divine rights of people. As a committed community, these values incorporate the New Afrikan Creed, the Seven Commandments of Umoja, the Nguzo Saba and the Instructions of Ptahhotep. Jegna values also *MAAT,* the Kemetic principle of balance and harmony which is represented as the Goddess who judges all persons desiring to successfully enter into the Afterlife, and outlines seven cardinal virtues. Truth, justice, propriety, harmony, balance, reciprocity, and order must also be imbibed into the essence of the beings initiated. These and other revolutionary principles are the standards by which we hold ourselves accountable.

The Way of the Elders

The first thing that can be said about eldership is that advanced age does not make one an elder. Let us admit that any older person is entitled to a certain amount of deference, courtesy, and respect but eldership is of a different order. According to Professor Fu-Kiau and others well-versed in sacred African tradition, eldership by its very nature implies initiation. In this sense, initiation means admission for instruction on the deeper, often hidden meanings of the external knowledge of a people. However, this admission presupposes that a definite, palpable connection be established with the Power or Powers that govern our lives. In the African framework, every one of us belongs to a spiritual lineage that originates from one of the great cosmic Powers called *neters* among the ancient Kemmiu, *rabs* among the Lebu, *abosum* among the

Akan, *vodun* among the Ewe and Fon, and *orishas* among the Yoruba. At the very least, one who would be an elder must be in direct communion with and representative of the Ancestors who, though inhabiting an invisible world, are bound to us by an unbreakable link and influence the course of our lives.

Eldership also implies responsibility; elders take responsibility for what happens in a community. Elders by definition are teachers, guides, and healers. The longer an elder lives, the more knowledge and, hopefully, wisdom he or she acquires. Such knowledge and wisdom must be put to the service of the family, community, people, and nation. For example, women who become elders actually acquire more power *after* their menses has stopped; that is, when their energies are no longer dedicated to childbirth and rearing. They become veritably the wise women of the community and often the most powerful personages resident. Elders also derive their power from their growing proximity to the Ancestors as they near the end of life. In traditional African life, so much prestige attaches to the role of the elder that when a child in a traditional community is asked what he (or she) wants to become in life, the answer is invariably an elder!

It goes without saying that an elder in an African community is one who, at the price of one's own life, protects a community's people, land, and culture. So, an elder is one who is prepared by, identified with and connected to the community, validated by the community, and is committed unconditionally to the community. While individual accomplishments of wealth, power and prestige may be admired, eldership is a community status and has attendant obligations.

Levels of Initiation: *Giri So, Benne So, Bolo So, So Dayi*
Initiation in our tradition is a lifelong experience with a specific time period for the rites of passage. The levels of initiation are a symbolic acknowledgment of the sojourn. These

rites at specific points allow the entire Afrikan community to participate in this acknowledgment and validation of the destiny one has before that community. Initiation is serious and it is complex. It is identification of one's spiritual linkage manifested in spirit, words, and actions.

For the Jegna Collective, initiation is a ritual and commitment to personhood. It is the communal acknowledgment of one's journey to reclaim and reinvigorate our tradition of excellence, deep thought, and service. We do not become Jegna through any series of rituals or work. Jegna is our personhood. It is not a title assigned by the community; it is our consciousness and heart. It is a description of persons in our community and the purpose they have been guided to fulfill by the Creator and the Ancestors. The Jegnoch Circle is the communal manifestation of that personhood. Through the levels of initiation we can from time to time, welcome, encourage and support persons on that path. In essence, this is their journey whether or not a Collective exists.

As a Collective, we have associated our levels of initiation with the Dogona ways of knowing. We have identified critical manifestations of knowing to "who we are as Afrikans," "where we are as Afrikans," "when we are as Afrikans," and "how we are as Afrikans." Within this contextual frame, we pursue the following four degrees of initiation:

Giri so – "word at face value," which confers that the initiate has learned a primary level of knowledge;

Benne so – "word on the side," which confers that the initiate has extended the range of knowledge acquired;

Bolo so – "word from behind (or preceding word)," which confers that the initiate has increased the depth and breadth of knowledge acquired;

So dayi – "clear word," which confers that the initiate has acquired a completely ordered and clarified level of knowledge.[2]

CHAPTER 2: THE JEGNA AS A COMMUNITY
OF EXCELLENCE by Dr. Itihari Toure

These four levels of initiation, construed from our study of the Dogon, comprise such a rich source of knowledge acquisition and identity development that they provide the support and depth with which Afrikan people can renew our sense of education as this process has meant since the days of the Ancestors. Therefore, the role of the Jegna Collective is to encourage through community and support each initiate's understanding of knowledge gained through "The Commons" experience.[3] Those who convene the Collective are responsible for its implementation. Those who are Sebai (the faculty) are responsible for the teaching and content. Those who are elders are responsible for the Collective's authenticity and accuracy regarding what is reawakened.

The current work of the Jegna Collective involves the curriculum of instruction to accompany each level of passage (initiation) in one's spiritual journey.

Summary of Experiences

The education process of the Jegna Collective occurs in several experiences: Afrientation, The (Monthly) Commons, The Transformation Institute (*Nsaka Sunsum*), The Jegna Collective Newsletter, The Sankofa Journeys, John Henrik Clarke Commemoration and Rituals, and since 2007, The Asa G. Hilliard III Annual Commemoration: To Be an Afrikan Teacher Institute.

As we continue to undertake our journey—especially as this sojourn involves us collectively—we sustain our recognition of the foundationally important efforts to which Asa Grant Hilliard III Nana Baffour Amankwatia II gave his life's energies. The Jegna Collective looks toward the day when all Afrikan people worldwide live within the realm of *So dayi*— clearly ordered in our knowledge and our actions, and embracing the education of our children in this fashion.

References

Ani, M. (Mwalimu A. Bomani Baruti). (October 28, 2012). *Dr. Marimba Ani discusses warriors.* Retrieved from http://www.youtube.com/watch?v=zrWoq11uz0Q

Fu-Kiau, K. (2003). *Self-healing power and therapy: Old teachings from Africa.* Baltimore: Black Classic Press.

Gallman, B., Ani., M., & Williams, L. (Eds.). (2003). *To be Afrikan: Essays by Africans in the process of Sankofa: Returning to the source.* Atlanta: MAAT.

Hilliard, A. G. (2002). *African power: Affirming African indigenous socialization in the face of the culture wars.* Gainesville, FL: Makare Publishing.

Hilliard, A. G., Williams, L., & Damali, N. (1987). *The teachings of Ptahhotep: The oldest book in the world.* Atlanta: Blackwood Press.

Nobles, W., & Nobles, Z. (November 15, 2001). *Nsaka Sunsum (Touching the spirit): A pedagogy and process of Black educational excellence. Multicultural Learning and Teaching,(6)2,* doi: 10.2202/2161-2412.1076

Toure, I. (2012). The way of the Jegna: Restoring excellence in African education. *African American Learners. 1*(1). Retrieved from https://isaac.wayne.edu/research/journal/article.php?newsletter=123&article=1700.

Chapter 3: Education and Culture in Context: The Case for an African-centered Approach

By Chike Akua

The Voice of the Children

At the end of every school year after my students completed their final exam I wrote them a letter, displaying it on the board. The letter read something like this:

> *Dear Brothers & Sisters:*
>
> It has been a privilege and a blessing to teach you this year. I hope you remember the lessons from the Book of Life more so than those in the textbook. I know you will leave here and do great things. I know you will transform the world into a place of peace for all and make the Ancestors proud. Have a safe and blessed summer.
>
> In Spirit & Truth,
> *Mr. Akua*

Then I had my students write me individual letters. They had to tell me about the most important thing they learned over the course of the year. It did not have to be an academic lesson, it could be a life lesson that they learned and felt was important. I gave them this last assignment for two reasons: 1) I felt it was important for them to reflect on all they had learned over the course of the year, and 2) I wanted to know what impacted them most about *how* I taught and *what* I taught. The following letters are a few among dozens my students have written me over the years that answered these two questions.

The letters serve as a kind of evidence of the effects of using African-centered methods.

Dear Mr. Akua:

> *In all of our lives we come across people who inspire and teach us in miraculous, unimaginable ways. You are one of those people to me! You are one of few examples of what appears to be a well put together man who has both purpose and unlimited promise. I can only hope that I can aid my younger brother in becoming a person with your values, insight, knowledge, and mentality.*
>
> *If throughout your teaching career you ever feel as if you may not be making a difference, re-read this card. I have spoken with faculty and staff from administration to guidance about you. Everyone has the utmost respect for you and wish all the best for you. The pupils that you have taught have also been inspired by you. Some students who have never enjoyed English or other people's cultures now are eagerly anticipating learning more.*
>
> *What have you done for me? You have introduced me to a new awareness. I have for a long time had a problem with authoritative figures. The knowledge that you gave to me allows me to now recognize this problem, among others, and search for ways to ameliorate them. In my search for Oneness with God, you have been a tool through which knowledge and, more importantly, wisdom has been gained.*
>
> *It has been said that if you make a difference in one person's life that you have conquered the world. You have definitely made the right choice*

CHAPTER 3: EDUCATION AND CULTURE IN CONTEXT: THE CASE FOR AN AFRICAN-CENTERED APPROACH
By Chike Akua

[to become a teacher]—not that you doubted this at any moment—and should continue to serve mankind by spreading your knowledge to its children.

I wish you all of the good fortune that you deserve. There should be more teachers in this world who truly want to make a difference and are interested in being instructors instead of babysitters. I will continue to pray for you and ask that you do the same [for me]. Hopefully, my little brother will be inspired by an African American man like you and also achieve greatness. Have a happy graduation and a wonderful, fulfilling life.

Camisha (12th Grade)
[from my six-week high school student teaching experience]

Mr. Akua,

I will understand if you do not remember me, but my name is Tirrell D. I had the distinct pleasure of having you educate me at Stephenson Middle School during the 1998-1999 school year.

To be very honest, I was web browsing recently and decided to type in your name. What I found was nothing short of amazing. I was so inspired to see that the Language Arts teacher that I looked up to so much in 7th grade is doing so much good in the world. I will not hesitate to say that you are one of the reasons why I went to college and majored in Education.

Today I teach 9th grade College Prep and Honors students at Mill Creek High School. I just wanted to send you an email and say that not only have you impacted my life in a major way, but I also use lessons and ideals you taught me over 10 years ago in my classroom.

Tirrell D.

Hi Mr. Akua:
 My name is Brittany Stewart. I was in your 7th grade class at Stephenson Middle School. You taught me reading and English a few years ago. I am now a senior at Stephenson High School. I hope that you remember who I am because you were someone I could never forget! You have made such an impact on my life and the lady that I have become! I just wanted to thank you for all of the wonderful things that you have given to me!
 I can remember conversations alone that forced me to do better, to want better and to know that I deserve better. To me you are the ideal person, the perfect role model for anyone, young or old. You are so giving and ask for nothing in return. I know I have a lot to learn and still quite young to the world, but I feel as though I have an advantage because I had you as a teacher.
 I am not sure yet about what school I plan on attending but I know I plan to major in education so I can have as big of an impact on someone's life as you did on mine. I love you so much and consider it a blessing to have known you!

Brittany Stewart
P.S. I forgot to thank you for the confidence you have given me because it has truly made a difference!

CHAPTER 3: EDUCATION AND CULTURE IN CONTEXT: THE CASE FOR AN AFRICAN-CENTERED APPROACH
By Chike Akua

Dear Mr. Akua:

It has been a pleasure having you as a teacher throughout this year. You taught me how to deal with certain situations and how to be a better person, in general. I will take this knowledge with me, use it, and spread it among many people. I've learned to "display my intelligence, not my ignorance," how to get into the proper mindset to learn, and how to handle responsibility. Those are the important things in life.

This has been my best year in school, maybe not grade-wise, but in learning wisdom and not as much book knowledge. Our relationship went past student-teacher, but to father-son and friend to friend. I appreciate that. You know I have no father. It's a joy when I can talk and chill with a teacher and picture him being my father.

You gave me the key to my past and future, but now I must open it and explore the things in it. All the things you taught about Black history were and are not taken for granted by me. I enjoyed learning that the most. One quality you have is that you are always ready to learn, even from a student. When somebody has that attitude, I am glad to be able to associate with them.

Your Student,
Philip (7th grade)

November 1993
Dear Mr. Akua:

Asta lama lakeum [As-salaam alaikum: Arabic for "peace be unto you." Kamau thought I was Muslim]. I know that I'll never be able to finish school. Because I want to learn but because of my Dad giving me mental and sometimes physical abuse, my mom is going to try and get me to see a school psychologist because it is stopping me from learning a bit. That is why I get angry so quick. But I'm sorry for snapping at you. Do I need to make up any assignments?

Your favorite 4th period student,
Kamau (8th grade)

*Kamau wrote me 10 years later. His emailed letter as an adult is below.

Dear Mr. Akua:

It was by God's grace that I was able to locate you using Yahoo web search. It has been 10 years since I was in your class at Hines Middle School located in Newport News, Virginia. I am writing this letter to let you know just how much being in your class 10 years ago changed my life and made me a better person. I am now 24 and I have two beautiful daughters: Dianna and Aaliyah. Their ages are 5 and 3. I am currently a student at Thomas Nelson Community college. I am transferring to Old Dominion University in the fall to get a degree in education.

CHAPTER 3: EDUCATION AND CULTURE IN CONTEXT: THE CASE FOR AN AFRICAN-CENTERED APPROACH
By Chike Akua

I distinctly remember being in your class, being a clown, disruptive, and sometimes ignorant of my choice of words and how and when I used them affected others. I remember when you would say, "Kamau, I need you to stay after class." I just knew I was being written up. But your methods of discipline didn't result in being sent to the principal's office.

You had a better punishment: an informative discussion. At my age now, I no longer see those discussions as punishment. It was those discussions that in the end made me the man who now loves life and cherishes every moment of it. My story 10 years ago was that I had a father that left me when my mother decided to get a divorce. I never had a father figure after that. Before the divorce took place, I would act out and cut up in school just to get a rise out of my peers. At the time I didn't know the value of an education. I do now and it's because of a teacher that really made me understand that I could do anything I put my mind to. Sadly, some students that were in my class that didn't take warning to your words are either in jail, dead, or strung out on drugs. I saw to it that I would not become a statistic, because I had the guidance of an educator who showed me that the path I was going would make me end up in one of those places.

Eventually I would end up losing focus of the tasks at hand which were my studies at school. I used acting out as a way to suppressing my problems at home. But you saw through it like glass even though you maybe never experienced what I had been going through. You made me see the bigger picture: that the actions of my parents, and the knowledge from an educator would define who I would become.

I learned the true meaning of the words "knowledge of self." This is a process when you read books to learn about things to gain knowledge for personal reasons—to define your ancestry and African American heritage. A teacher once said, "Not everything in these textbooks is accurate, but it's up to you as an individual to find out the real deal on your own."

I just want to say thank you for the opportunity to be a student in your class and learn how to become a young man. It is because of you, Mr. Akua, that I chose a career as an educator. You were an inspiring educator that actually cared and loved your students as your own children. You never gave up on us, even the students who acted out like me.

I want to become a leader for black youth. Someone has to show them that there's more to life than driving a Hummer, selling drugs to our own people, and having kids at a young age. I just want you to know that you do make a difference and I appreciate all that you taught me as a youth 10 years ago. I had thoughts as a youth that you didn't care and you put up with me for a paycheck. In all actuality, you really did care and it shows through me and this letter. I stand here before you humbly to say that because of you, Mr. Akua, I am a better young black man and human being.

Peace and Blessings,
Kamau

Culture and Education in Context

The earliest documented system of education had its genesis in the Nile Valley of Africa. Their system of education produced a people, a society, buildings, structures, monuments, and a high level of science whose sophistication has yet to be fully understood or surpassed (Hilliard, 1995).

In addition, the result of their system of education led to origins, innovations, and expertise in reading and writing, language and literature, agriculture and astronomy, architecture and engineering, mathematics and medicine, philosophy and physics, science and technology, to name a few (Finch, 1998). The place was called Kemet and is today referred to as Egypt. Kemet was nourished and nurtured significantly, both culturally and spiritually, by its neighbor to the South, Nubia (Browder, 1992). It is in the Nile Valley of Africa that we encounter one of the first terms relative to teaching and learning—the word *seba*.

(seba) "door"
(seba) "star"
(seba) "teach", "teaching"

Seba, in the language of *medu netcher* (often referred to by the Greek term *hieroglyphics*) actually has three primary meanings: "teach," "door," and "star" (Obenga, 2000). It is in the construction and connotation of this word that we find the ancient African philosophy of education: "The teacher opens the door to the universe so that the student may shine like a star." *Seba* came to refer also to the deep thought and wisdom of the wise and learned. The Master Teacher in ancient Kemet was often referred to as *Seba* (Hilliard, 1997).

Four thousand five hundred years ago (2500 B.C.E.), the ancient teacher, sage, and scribe Ptahhotep, who has written the world's oldest complete text, gives us a definition of what a Seba does and what a Seba is known by:

> The Seba (wise person/Master Teacher) feeds the Ka (soul) with what endures...the wise is known by his good actions. The heart of the wise matches his or her tongue and his or her lips are straight when he or she speaks. The wise have eyes that are made to see and ears that are made to hear what will profit the offspring. (Hilliard, Williams, & Damali, 1987, p. 32)

> "The educational process was not seen only as acquiring knowledge; it was seen as a process of transformation."
> -Dr. Wade Nobles

In addition to this ambitious definition of a teacher, there was a vast and distinct body of literature which instructed people in the way of the Master Teacher. The teachings were referred to as the *Sebait* (pronounced *say-by-eet*), wisdom texts or the books of wise instruction (Karenga, 1984). Wade Nobles observes that in ancient African schools, "The educational process was not seen only as acquiring knowledge; it was seen as a PROCESS OF TRANSFORMATION of the learner or initiate, who progressed through successive stages of **rebirth to become EXCELLENT**" (Hilliard & Payton-Stewart, 1990, p. 13). In addition to mastery of practical skills, this process was typified by the *whmy msw* (pronounced *we-he-mee me-su*), a re-awakening or rebirth into higher consciousness (Hilliard, 1997).

So this ancient African education was a cyclical process of initiation and transformation. When Nile Valley Africans migrated to West Africa, they reproduced the same philosophical conception of the nature of the child, the student, and each child's potential (Maiga, 1992). Each child was seen as a rising sun and a radiating center of light with tremendous power and energy (Fu-Kiau, 2003).

> "In west Africa, each child was seen as a rising sun and a radiating center of light..."

The Kemetic description of the ancient Master Teacher is not only a far cry from what is expected of teachers today it is based in a philosophy that is not understood or illuminated in most Western schools of education where teachers are trained. In addition, the description of the child/student as a rising sun and radiating center of light is not understood or illuminated, either. In short, those who teach African American children, in most cases, have not consulted our most traditional and consistent ancient examples of expertise or our most contemporary examples of excellence.

Now, fast-forward 4,500 years from the ancient to the modern. In the first essay of *Young, Gifted, and Black: Promoting High Achievement Among African-American Students*, Theresa Perry located the African American philosophy of education. After examining the writings of Frederick Douglass, Harriet Jacobs, Malcolm X, Ben Carson, Joycelyn Elders, Gwendolyn Parker, Haki Madhubuti, Septima Clark, and Maya Angelou, a definite pattern with conscious consistency emerged: a theme of "freedom for literacy and literacy for freedom, racial uplift, citizenship, and leadership" (Perry, Steele, & Hilliard, 2003, p. 10). Then, as now, "the major function of education is to help secure the survival of a people" (Wilson, 1991, p. 1).

In other words, the purpose of education was to secure freedom and freedom brought with it the right to a proper education. Education inculcated within the student a responsibility to improve the plight of one's people. It is the underlying ethos and essence of the pursuit of education for Black people in America. However, the African American philosophy of education is not isolated; rather, it is a clear and compelling cultural thread in a broader tapestry, an extension of the ancient African philosophy of education and a matter of practical survival for our culture and our people.

Education and socialization have always been a top priority for African people whether in ancient and independent times or in the context of *Maafa*, the intentional, catastrophic interruption of African civilization characterized by enslavement, colonization, castration, miseducation, economic manipulation, lynching, rape, family separation, etc. (Ani, 1980).

Prior to integration, even in the midst of dilapidated buildings, a diabolically unequal distribution of funds, and secondhand textbooks, the desire for and pursuit of education was clear and consistent among Black people. In addition, parent meetings were packed with caregivers who insisted on the best education and preparation possible for their children (Siddle Walker, 2000). Those who know this narrative sit in awe, wonder, disappointment, and disillusionment when examining the state of education for African Americans today. If this standard of excellence was the case prior to integration, what happened?

There is another story. There is a little known narrative as to why far too many of our schools are not producing the excellence we expect or desire. With the onset of integration in the 1960s and 1970s, many white educational leaders in an effort to skirt the mandates of the *Brown v. Board of Education* decision of 1954, began to get rid of Black teachers and administrators.

> Pre-integration black teachers and administrators produced a track record of excellence without excuses, dignity and integrity regardless of resources.

Today, over 70% of urban school teachers are white and female in schools where students are overwhelmingly children of color (Fenwick, 2001). Many teachers today exhibit what Joyce King calls dysconscious racism, an uncritical habit of mind that accepts the status quo as a given (King, 1991). Because of the inherent, uncritical acceptance of inequity, dysconsciousness prevents the active pursuit of social justice. It creates more than apathy; it creates cooperation with educational oppression. However, pre-integration Black teachers and administrators produced a track record of excellence without excuses, dignity, and integrity regardless of resources, and maintained a curricular thrust toward cultural excellence and social justice (Siddle Walker, 2000).

In the wake of the *Brown* decision, the Black teacher workforce was decimated. Over 39,000 Black teachers and leaders were the victims of "dismissals, demotions, forced resignations, 'non-hiring,' token promotions, reduced salaries, [and] diminished responsibilities" (Fultz, 2004, p. 14). The proportion of African American teachers and administrators to Caucasian teachers and administrators "declined to less than half of what it was before 'integration'" (Hilliard, 1997, p. 60).

All of this was done in the name of complying with the *Brown* decision. However, it led one observer to note that it "is not *integration;* rather it is *disintegration* [emphasis in the original]" (Fultz, 2004, p. 14). Indeed, Black schools slowly disintegrated along with the high standards of achievement. In light of this, it is important to note that recent low numbers of African American teachers is not accidental, but *intentional.* Perhaps this is why John Henrik Clarke notes with sober and systematic incisiveness, "the powerful will never educate the powerless to take their power from them" (Browder, 1992).

CHAPTER 3: EDUCATION AND CULTURE IN CONTEXT: THE CASE FOR AN AFRICAN-CENTERED APPROACH
By Chike Akua

> "The powerful will never educate the powerless to take their power from them."
> -Dr. John Henrik Clarke

Black children were sent to "integrated" schools which did not foster the ancient African or African American philosophy of education. By and large, their caring teachers who demanded excellence without excuses were no longer present. As a result, over the past several decades, African American children have been sliding down a slippery slope, resulting in alien identity and underachievement. The *2010 Schott 50 State Report on Black Males in Education* indicated that the national Black male graduation rate was a mere 47% (Jackson & Holzman, 2010). Some school systems had Black male graduation rates as low as an appalling 22%. Moreover, many urban schools are struggling with increased incidents of classroom management problems and violence. Clearly, the current system of education is not working.

This is the backdrop against which many teachers enter the teacher workforce. Many enter it not knowing what caused the seemingly daunting day-to-day challenges they face as they try to reach and teach children in urban schools. Experienced and veteran teachers also witness the year-to-year erosion of any semblance of excellence. Often the children and their parents are blamed without a contextualized understanding of the socio-cultural forces that have been imposed upon them.

But even with these devastating challenges, many African American schools, teachers, and students have upheld the standard of excellence that was once so common. Unfortunately, their stories are not used often enough as examples of what is possible.

> This chapter is for those who wish to recapture the an-cient African and African American philosophy of educational excellence and effectively put it into practice. It is about results.

This chapter is for those who are interested in solutions that go far beyond minimal competency tests. It is for those who understand that systemic certification and college degrees are not enough. It is for those who wish to recapture the ancient African and African American philosophy of education and effectively put it into practice. This is education for transformation. It is this tradition "that made us respected as teachers all over the globe" (Gallman, Ani, & Williams, 2003, p. 61). This chapter is about results. It is about my transformational experiences of attempting to recapture and reproduce the ancient African and African American philosophy of education as I put it into practice in my almost 20 years as an educator.

For those educators who teach mixed populations of students and may be wondering if the methods described here are too ethnically centered, please be mindful of the thoughtful words of Carol Lee: "'Once we learn to teach poor Black children, we will likely learn better how to educate all children'" (King, 2005, p. xxvi).

CHAPTER 3: EDUCATION AND CULTURE IN CONTEXT: THE CASE FOR AN AFRICAN-CENTERED APPROACH
By Chike Akua

I have taught in urban schools and suburban schools, predominantly Black schools and schools with mixed populations and diversity. I have taught high-achieving students on the accelerated track and students who were below grade level; students whose behavior was exemplary and students whose behavior and socialization required acute and immediate attention, intervention, and modification. I have also taught students labeled with every undesirable acronym. I have taught in situations where 22 out of 24 of my homeroom students had a parole officer.

> "I have taught in situations where 22 out of 24 of my homeroom students had a parole officer.

In addition, I have had the opportunity to travel around the country speaking at conferences and coaching teachers and leaders in public, charter, and private schools. I have spoken at parent meetings and school assemblies for students, addressing hundreds of students at a time in some of of the most challenged communities and challenging schools. I have observed that there are startling and crippling similarities in America's public schools relative to the achievement of Black children. But there is good news, too. The challenges many teachers and schools are facing can be repaired. Hilliard notes, "Evaluation research shows that extraordinarily high achievement gains can be made, in a relatively brief period, by relatively simple approaches, in spite of typical challenges, for the lowest-income students, regardless of race" (Perry, Hilliard, & Steele, 2003, p. 144).

What Is African-centered Education (ACE)?

In my research and practice, I have noted that there are four major tenets of African-centered education. First, ACE places Africa, African people, and African points of view at the **center** of all things studied. This means that students themselves, their community, and their perspectives are valued and become the lens through which they view the world.

Second, ACE helps students critically examine how the subject or object of study is related to the image and interests of Africa and African people. To paraphrase a basic, essential question that Dr. John Henrik Clarke has posed: Is it good for African people? If this simple, yet profound question is posed to children and they are shown how to back up their answer with at least three compelling pieces to their argument, then we will raise up children who are critically thinking and culturally conscious persons.

Third, ACE requires methods that are unique and indigenous to the nature and needs of African children. In other words, the way knowledge is structured, presented, and engaged is different from the traditional "stand and deliver," "sit and get" paradigm of education in which too many teachers and students are languishing. So ACE is not just about learning African history and it is not just about content; it is also about the method of delivery. ACE methods use, among other things, bodily-kinesthetic movement; call-and-response; movement and dance; music, rhythm, and drumming; reflection and practical application, to name a few examples.

Fourth, ACE requires what Asante calls, "a consciousness of victory" (1980). This means that despite the horrific atrocities that African people have suffered, there needs to be an understanding that African people are resilient and triumphant—not defined by circumstance, *refined* by circumstance. This consciousness of victory should permeate every lesson and every classroom activity, leading to a transformative vocation in which our children serve their family, their community, and humanity.

References

Ani, M. (1980). *Let the circle be unbroken: The implications of African spirituality in the diaspora.* Lawrenceville, NJ: Red Sea Press.

Asante, M. (1980). *Afrocentricity: The theory of social change.* Buffalo, NY: Amulefi Publishing.

Browder, A. T. (1992). *Nile Valley contributions to civilization.* Washington, DC: Institute of Karmic Guidance.

Fenwick, L. T. (2001). *Patterns of excellence: Policy perspectives on diversity in teaching and school leadership.* Atlanta: Southern Education Foundation.

Finch, C. S. (1998). *The star of deep beginnings.* Decatur, GA: Khenti.

Fu-Kiau, K. (2003). *Self-healing power and therapy: Old teachings from Africa.* Baltimore: Black Classic Press.

Fultz, M. (Spring, 2004). The displacement of Black educators post-"Brown": An overview and analysis. *History of Education Quarterly, 44*(1): 11-45.

Gallman, B., Ani, M., & Williams, L. (2003). *To be Afrikan: Essays by Africans in the process of Sankofa: Returning to the source.* Atlanta: MAAT.

Hilliard, A. G. (1995). *The Maroon within us: Selected essays in African-American community socialization.* Baltimore: Black Classic Press.

Hilliard, A. G. (1997). *SBA: The reawakening of the African mind.* Gainesville, FL: Makare Publishing.

Hilliard, A. G., & Payton-Stewart, L. (1990). *The infusion of African and African American content in the school curriculum: Proceedings of the first national conference, October 1989.* Morristown, NJ: Aaron Press.

Hilliard, A. G., Williams, L., & Damali, N. (1987). *The teachings of Ptahhotep: The oldest book in the world.* Atlanta: Blackwood Press.

Jackson, J., & Holzman, M. (2010). *Yes we can, the Schott 50 state report on public education and Black males.* Cambridge, MA: Schott Foundation for Public Education. Retrieved from http://www.schott foundation.org/publications/schott-2010-black-male-report.pdf

Karenga, M. (1984). *Selections from the Husia: Sacred wisdom of ancient Egypt.* Los Angeles: University of Sankore Press.

King, J. (Ed.). (2005). *Black education: A transformative research and action agenda for the new century.* Mahwah, NJ: Lawrence Erlbaum Associates.

Maïga, B. (1992). *L'éducation du jeune enfant d'âge prescoline au Mali.* (Doctoral dissertation). Strasbourg, France: University of Strasbourg.

Obenga, T. (2000). *African philosophy during the period of the Pharoahs, 2800-330 BC.* London: Karnak House.

Perry, T., Hilliard, A. G., & Steele, C. (2003). *Young, gifted, and Black: Promoting high achievement among African-American students.* Boston: Beacon Press.

Siddle Walker, V. (Autumn, 2000). Valued segregated schools for African American children in the South, 1935-1969: A review of common themes and characteristics. *Review of Educational Research, 70*(3): 253-285.

Wilson, A. (1991). *Awakening the natural genius of Black children.* Bronx, NY: Afrikan World Infosystems.

Chapter 4: Spirituality and Leadership in the Afrikan Church in North America

By Reverend Dr. Mark A. Lomax

Introduction

Since the formation and institutionalization of Afrikan churches in North America there has been dis-ease in the Afrikan Zion. The dis-ease issues from the fact that far too many Afrikan-descended Christian leaders in North America all too often teach and preach the Bible as if it has nothing to say about the lived experiences of oppressed Afrikan peoples. While I certainly do not intend to minimize the valiant leadership provided by the legions of leaders in the Afrikan Church in North America who sacrificed and served with courage, vision, and distinction in various ways and through various churches and denominations, I want to make the point that the Gospel of God through Jesus the Christ is, if nothing else about setting captives free.

While no one can deny the valiant role that many Afrikan descended leaders in North America have played in abolishing systemic forms of oppression through various protests and rebellions there remains, to no small degree, a self-hatred and a self-deprecating consciousness among far too many Afrikan followers of the Christ. Why? I believe it has everything to do with the way we as teachers, preachers, and leaders in the Afrikan Church image both God and the Christ of God; fail to take our own agency seriously as we come to the texts of Scripture and the governance of the Church; and insist on replicating the liturgical practices of our historic oppressors. The questions are: What is this freedom that is so integral to the gospel of Jesus the Christ? Can any oppressed person who subscribes uncritically to the theologies, liturgies, and forms of governance of her or his oppressor ever truly attain that freedom? At a deeper level, the questions might be: Why are Afrikan Christians in North America so enamored with European theological principles, governance, and liturgical practices on the one hand, and so disparaging of Afrikan theological principles, governance, and liturgical practices on the other? What is it that Afrikans in North America find so compelling about everything European and so repulsive about all things Afrikan? These are not new questions.

In the past century alone Afrikan-descended pastors, scholars, and leaders have challenged European ideological and theological hegemony in the Afrikan Church in North America. Bishop Henry McNeal Turner was among the first to argue for and develop the notion that "God is a Negro" (1895; Cross, 2003). Similarly, Marcus Mosiah Garvey argued, "if, as established Christian churches preached, man was made in the image and likeness of God, then black men should depict a God in their own image and likeness, which would inevitably be black."[1] Professor Robert E. Hood in his book *Must God Remain Greek? Afro Cultures and God-Talk* raised the following questions: "Do Christians from Third World cultures have to become imitation Europeans or imitation North Americans before they can be considered fitting contributors to the formation and shaping of Christian thought? Must they steadily continue to contribute to their own *invisibility* within Christian thought by surrendering traditions and cultures long dismissed as 'pagan,' 'animistic,' 'heathen,' and 'polytheistic'?"[2] Josiah U. Young in the introduction to his book *Black and African Theologies: Siblings or Distant Cousins?* states:

> The major task of African theologians is to
> expose continuities and discontinuities be-
> tween African traditional religion and Chris-
> tian faith. . . . This study upholds the view
> that there is ground for a future alignment
> between black theologians of the United
> States and Africa. Inasmuch as black theo-
> logians in both places share similarities,
> black liberation themes might join with
> themes of African indigenization in a theol-
> ogy relevant to Africa and its Diaspora. To
> gether they might render valuable service to
> the poor and thus to the gospel.[3]

Dwight Hopkins and George Cummings studied slave narratives in their book *Cut Loose Your Stammering Tongue: Black
Theology in the Slave Narratives* and attempted to distill out
of the slave narratives the core beliefs of enslaved Afrikan
peoples in North America. Hopkins, Cummings, and others
discovered that many enslaved Afrikans in North America
"took the remnants of their traditional religious structures and
meshed them together with their interpretation of the Bible."[4]
Finally, Dr. Will Coleman in his book *Tribal Talk: Black Theology, Hermeneutics, and African American Ways of "Telling the Story,"* set forth the argument, particularly in the first
chapter, that the deep religious thought of Afrikan peoples is
foundational for Afrikans living and doing theology in the
Diaspora. It seems then, that every so often God sends a messenger to Afrikan peoples in an effort to call them home spiritually.

Yet, we are not saved. We are not saved, nor are we
free because there is persistent dis-ease of self-hatred and self-
deprecation in the Afrikan Zion. We are not saved and we are
not free because the vision of our God is obscured by our
collective unwillingness to see our God with our own eyes.

41

Though many of the external chains of oppression have been broken, far too many of us remain bound to notions of God, culture, and community that are not our own.

This failure to see our God or, put another way, to see ourselves in God, is not limited to Afrikan-descended peoples. Women of all descriptions have struggled with and continue to struggle with a similar disease; but Afrikan women have borne and bear a triple burden. Not only is the Bible radically patriarchal in regard to the way it images God, many if not most interpreters of the Bible whether male or female have brought and bring their sexism to the text with them. Further, the question of economic location especially in relation to women is seldom raised by either pastors or other church leaders.

Several scholars have addressed these concerns. Dr. Jacquelyn Grant in *White Women's Christ and Black Women's Jesus: Feminist Christology and Womanist Response* addressed the issue of Christology and argued, "Black feminism grows out of Black women's tri-dimensional reality of race/sex/class. It holds that full human liberation cannot be achieved simply by the elimination of any one form of oppression."[5] During a discussion on Alice Walker's *The Color Purple,* Dr. Delores S. Williams says in *Sisters in the Wilderness: The Challenge of Womanist God-Talk,* "The idea of the divine spirit working within humans is more efficacious for women's development of self-worth than notions of God in male or female form."[6] These women and a host of others like Cheryl A. Kirk-Duggan, Kelly Brown-Douglas, Teresa Fry-Brown, and Renita Weems-Espinoza to name just a few, re-image God so as to wrest God from the deadly clutches of patriarchy while simultaneously attending to the issues of race and class. Yet there remains dis-ease in the Afrikan Zion and we are not saved. How might we be saved? What is the cure for our dis-ease? What will empower our wellness spiritually and culturally?

CHAPTER 4: SPIRITUALITY AND LEADERSHIP IN THE AFRIKAN CHURCH IN NORTH AMERICA
By Reverend Dr. Mark A. Lomax

Spirit/Spirituality

Our salvation and our cure come from knowing who we are and what we are to do in the world. The questions of identity and purpose are at the heart of the problems confronting Afrikan-descended peoples both on the continent of Afrika and throughout the Afrikan Diaspora. Our collective proclivity toward everything European and/or American is inextricably tied to the vicious, ongoing *Maafa* (destruction) and the concomitant campaign to denigrate everything that is indigenous to Afrika, including her notions of God.

Everything in me is resisting the urge to lay many of the past and present problems in Afrika and among Afrikan people at the feet of the *Maafa* because of all of the voices that scream "get over it." Yet, neither I nor my people have gotten over it nor can we until confessions are made, forgiveness is sought and given, and significant reparations are paid. The dis-ease of Afrikan people cannot be cured with a wink and a smile and an invitation to the table of communalship to which all of God's children are invited to sit and to eat of the bounty of God's supply without ever truly acknowledging— to say nothing of addressing—the sin that prohibits true communalship, real communion. We need one another desperately—Afrikan and Asian and European. But our fathers and mothers ate sour grapes and our teeth are yet set on edge.

Well, you may ask, did not Jesus pay it all? Is it not all under the blood of the crucified Christ? Was it not all buried with him at his death? Did he not pay the needed restitution? Yes and no. All of our racism and prejudice, sexism and bigotry, classism and homophobia are under the blood if we have confessed and repented of our part in them; if, having confessed and repented we are walking in the newness of peace and unity with those who continue to be pushed to the margins of the global reality that is ours today. No, if we make excuses for ourselves; no, if we continue to deny our own culpability in the transgressions of our ancestors; no!

In truth our blackness or whiteness or redness or yellowish-ness are false categories. If we believe the biblical text, God created humankind in God's own "image, according to [God's] own likeness" (Genesis 1:26-27).[7] Further, the sexual categories we use to differentiate between male and female were not intended to separate the sexes, but to unify them. The Divine idea, I believe, was and is for human beings to find a point of unity in their common origin—God.

For that reason there can be no question that every person is "spiritual." Though every people have and practice one or more forms of "spirituality" the essence, the vital life force, the core reality of human being is spirit.

From a biblical perspective the Gods (Heb. *Elohim*) said, "let us make humankind in our own image, according to our likeness. . . . So the Gods (*Elohim*) created humankind in God's image, in the image of God, God created them; male and female God created them."[8] Who were the Gods who created humankind and what was their form? Were they corporeal beings like the humans they created in their own "image and likeness" or were they spiritual beings analogous to contemporary notions of energy? If the former, where are they now or where did they go? If the latter, then in what sense are human beings created in their image and likeness? Of course, most readers of Scripture perceive the Gods as wholly spiritual beings who are ever-present though invisible to the naked eye and intangible to the human touch. Human beings therefore bear the image and likeness of the Gods in their essence or core. In that sense every person is spiritual.

The word for "God" in Genesis 1, *Elohim,* while plural is frequently translated by the singular noun "God." Though sometimes interpreted in its plural sense, it is most often used to convey what is called "the plural of majesty" and is inclusive of all deities (*American Jewish Yearbook,* NIBSD: CD-ROM). If this is true, then one must consider the fact that even female deities are subsumed under this appellation.

The second creation story in Genesis 2 drives the point home: "then the LORD God (*Yahweh Elohim*) formed man (Heb. *adam*) from the dust of the ground (*adamah*), and breathed into his nostrils the breath of life; and the man (*adam*) became a living being" (Genesis 2:7).[9] God formed the corporeal aspect of man (*adam*) using the dust (*adamah*) of the ground, a feminine element. The being man (*adam*) did not live until God (*Yahweh Elohim*) breathed into his nostrils the breath (*neshamah*) of life. The Hebrew word *neshamah* may also be translated by the English word "spirit." Again, the vital principle or life force in humankind is spirit. All people are spiritual from a biblical perspective. Human beings are spiritual precisely because their essential nature is spirit. Further, all people practice one or more forms of spirituality.

While the creation account in Genesis 2 separates the creation of the man from that of the woman, it also unifies male and female in a powerful way. Woman is depicted as being created from the rib of the man by God (vv. 21-22);[10] they are thereby made the perfect/complete complement of one another—so much so that they are to be "one flesh" (v. 24).[11]

In sum, spirituality must not be confused with religious expression or devotion. The former suggests an ontological reality—the essential nature of human being, which is spirit. The latter, religious expression or devotion, points toward a plethora of ways that human beings have sought and continue to seek an inner wholeness or peace. The inner wholeness or peace that human beings seek is a deeper awareness of and oneness with God—that invisible, intangible yet pervasive and ever present person(s) in whose image we have been made and whose breath/spirit (*neshamah*) has given us life. As spiritual beings humans routinely practice some form of spirituality; we cannot do otherwise. We are who we "be" and we "be" spiritual.

The creation stories cited above represent two different writers' ideas about the way humanity was created. It can first be argued that the creation accounts in Genesis 1 and 2 describe a one- and two-step process of the creation of human beings respectively. In Genesis 1 the Gods simply speak and humankind manifests. In Genesis 2 the "LORD GOD" (*Yahweh Elohim*) fashions a vessel, and then breathes the divine breath (*neshamah*) into it. In each case it is possible to assert that the person(s) whom God created were and are wholly spirit—from the inside out. Second, it can be argued that the spirit-flesh duality which comes to the fore in Christian thought primarily through the writings of the apostle Paul is more reflective of Hellenist philosophical notions than divine revelation (e.g., Platonic dualism). Positing such arguments flies in the face of Western or Constantinian Christianity because it does not permit one to determine who is or is not spiritual on the basis of his or her religious expression. Rather, it demands that every person see every other person as spiritual regardless of his or her religious heritage and/or practice. It is from the former perspective, however, that one must seek to provide leadership in the Afrikan Church of North America in the 21st century.

Jesus' Ministry as a Model for Leaders in the Afrikan Church

Generally speaking, the Afrikan Church of the 21st century exists within a multicultural, multiethnic, and multi-faith environment. She and her people also face impoverishment, disease, and various forms of oppression. Though enslavement and

CHAPTER 4: SPIRITUALITY AND LEADERSHIP IN THE AFRIKAN CHURCH IN NORTH AMERICA
By Reverend Dr. Mark A. Lomax

Jim Crow semi-slavery no longer exist by legal fiat, we find evidence of both the dis-ease's prominence in the Afrikan Zion and the continuing disparities between Afrikan and non-Afrikan Americans with the exception of First World/Native American peoples, in the following examples and circumstances: the privatization of the nation's prisons that hold a disproportionately high percentage of Afrikan men relative to their percentage of the American population; the re-segregation and under-funding of the nation's inner city public schools; the tragically high percentage of chronic illnesses of all descriptions among Afrikans in North America, along with the concomitant lack of affordable health care; and the continued disparity in salaries between European Americans and Afrikan Americans. Given the weight of verifiable evidence, no reasonable person could argue that the masses of Afrikan people in North America are better off than they were 50 years ago, even though it is also true that a larger percentage of Afrikan-descended people in North America now occupy the ranks of the American middle and upper economic classes.

Whereas it was once true that many of the most prominent leaders in the Afrikan Church in North America spoke with a prophetic voice and challenged the institutional structures of racism and classism through their demand for justice on the basis of Christian morality while simultaneously working with their own people to alleviate the pains to injustice, now, in all too many instances they stand on the proverbial sidelines of the playing field of justice, boldly collecting the meager resources of their own downtrodden people for their own personal benefit and for the buildings and houses they occupy. There are however a number, maybe even legions, of far less prominent and less influential leaders in the Afrikan Church in North America standing firmly and boldly in the traditions of their mothers and fathers. Without fanfare or public acclaim they serve the present age with courage and determination. Yet, we are not saved. The dis-ease remains in the Afrikan Zion. Why?

While the Afrikan Church in North America has an extremely vital witness to offer (i.e., the Gospel of God through Jesus the Christ), it can ill afford to be bigoted, sexist, classist, and judgmental with regard to the very people it has been called and sent by the Christ of God to evangelize. Rather, the Afrikan Church in North America must struggle and strive to become like its Lord—completely obedient to and focused on living and doing the will of God. That is no small task!

Jesus was the word of God incarnate precisely because he chose to listen to and obey God even to death on a cross. Jesus chose to listen to and obey God within a particular religious, social, political, cultural, economic, and historical reality. The religio-cultural and socio-political realities within which Jesus lived were Judaism and Roman colonialism. The economic and historical realities were poverty and Roman oppression, respectively. Given the religious, social, political, cultural, economic, and historical context in which he found himself, Jesus could have opted to identify with and choose the path of least resistance, the socio-religious way that was the safest, oft-trodden road that always leads to success within empire. Indeed, the devil is imaged as tempting Jesus to choose one or more these alternate routes (Matthew 4:1-11; Mark 1:13; Luke 4:1-13). Rather than choosing the way of the temple (i.e., institutionalized Judaism) or the way of assimilation into the Roman colonial matrix, Jesus chose a third way, the way of Godly obedience. This third way that Jesus chose for himself and for his followers was the most difficult by far. It was the way that led not just to his death but more importantly to his resurrection and glorification.

CHAPTER 4: SPIRITUALITY AND LEADERSHIP IN THE AFRIKAN CHURCH IN NORTH AMERICA
By Reverend Dr. Mark A. Lomax

All Christian leaders are called and sent by God to choose the third way—the way of Jesus, the way that leads to the cross and ultimately the resurrection. Before entering a discussion relative to what the third way might be for Christian leaders in the Afrikan Church in 21st-century North America, it is important to examine what choosing the third way might have meant for Jesus.

Jesus was committed to the same covenants his ancestors had with Yahweh—the Mosaic and Davidic covenants. Jesus was not legalistic. He grasped, internalized, and lived out of the spiritual principles embedded in the Law. In so doing, he never lost sight of his people—their foibles, their troubles and sorrows, their existential condition, and yes, their sins and transgressions. Jesus attended services at the synagogue each Sabbath day and participated in the annual festivals of his people. Jesus was grounded in the religion and culture of Israel despite the fact that Rome—the dominating political, economic, and military power of the day—was pervasive through its military, governance, culture, and religion.

Jesus was committed to the liberation of his people. While representatives of the Roman Empire occasionally sought his help, Jesus focused his energy and efforts on the people of Judaea-Israel. Indeed, Jesus was so focused in terms of the reach of his ministry that one must wonder whether he himself had an agenda that encompassed the whole world or whether his first-century followers developed such a purview.

Jesus was committed to speaking truth to power in the name of Yahweh. The representatives of the power structure to whom Jesus spoke included Scribes, Pharisees, and Sadducees, all of whom were both representatives of the Temple (institutional Judaism) and, by virtue of the fact that they did not challenge Roman dominance, of Empire.

Jesus was committed to maintaining his relationship with Yahweh. Time and again those who wrote the Gospels informed the reader of Jesus' habit of getting alone and praying.

Finally, Jesus was committed to giving his life for his people's freedom. Jesus gave his life for his people not only through death on the cross but most importantly for the purposes of this article, through a life lived for their benefit.

Contemporary leaders in the Afrikan Church in North America are called, I believe, to follow Jesus. Though there is no record of Jesus himself ever demanding that we worship him, we have chosen to worship rather than follow him. We must first therefore decide to follow him even as we worship our God in his name. But who is our God?

To speak of God using a color symbol like black may indeed be far too limiting of what I perceive to be the God reality. While such a symbol has been useful in the past, enough has now been written about Afrikan notions of God to re-member the God(s) of our ancestors. Further, while the color "black" might be limiting, it is liberating to know that Afrikan peoples possessed notions of God long before their encounters with Christianized Europeans. Afrikan notions of God were not wholly animistic nor were they in any way barbaric. They were different from, and in numerous ways similar to, the Judeo-Christian conception of God. For example, the ancient Egyptians, like most Afrikan peoples, possessed a dynamic mythic world long before Yahweh spoke to Moses at the burning bush.

Within the Egyptian cosmogony there was a single Creator or High God called Atum in Heliopolis, Ptah in Memphis, Amen in Thebes, and Re/Râ in Hermopolis. According to one creation account:

> In the beginning a great flood, known as the Nun or Nu, engulfed the universe. As in the Bible, the Creator's spirit caused the waters to stir, initiating the generative process. Out of the Nun arose the primeval hill and the self-created Creator. . . . Other deities, like angels in the Bible, were the creations of the one all-powerful deity, and each of the cult centers tried to argue that the Creator deities of the other cults were just lesser deities created by their own chief god.[12]

Sir E. A. Wallis Budge in the book *Egyptian Religion* offers another, though similar version of the creation.

> According to the writings of the Egyptians, there was a time when neither heaven nor earth existed, and when nothing had being except the boundless primeval water, which was, however, shrouded with thick darkness. . . . At length the spirit of the primeval water felt the desire for creative activity, and having uttered the word, the world sprang straightway into being in the form which had already been depicted in the mind of the spirit before he spake the word which resulted in its creation. The next act of creation was the formation of a germ, or egg, from which sprang Râ, the Sun-god, within whose shining form was embodied the almighty power of the divine spirit.[13]

These Egyptian creation stories were old by the time Joseph and subsequently Jacob-Israel entered Egypt. Are we to believe that the descendants of Jacob-Israel spent nearly 400 years in Egypt, Afrika and were left untouched by her notions of God, spirit, creation, the afterlife, anthropology, and so on? I think not! It is more than likely that all of the descendants of Jacob-Israel, perhaps especially Moses who was raised in the Pharaoh's house, were deeply influenced by ancient Egyptian religious ideas. I would argue that if God is in some sense "black" S/he is so because Black Afrikan peoples were among the first to receive and to communicate the Divine self-revelation.

Leaders in the Afrikan Church in North America should, I believe, study the religious ideas of ancient Afrika, especially Egypt, with at least as much dedication and zeal as we do those of Europe. This is particularly true of the myth of Osiris (Ausar), the Egyptian Deity of Resurrection.

There are several versions of the myth of Osiris. In short, Osiris was of divine origin; he suffered death and mutilation at the hands of his evil brother Set, he was buried and rose again and rules as king of the underworld and judge of the dead. Egyptians believed that because Osiris conquered death, the righteous Egyptian could also conquer death.[14] The myth of Osiris captivated the Egyptian mind and their devout attention throughout antiquity. Indeed, "they raised Osiris to such an exalted position in heaven that he became the equal and, in certain cases, the superior of Râ and ascribed to him the attributes which belong unto God."[15] As difficult as it may be for many Christians to accept, it is impossible to read the ancient myth of Osiris and fail to see its relationship to the life, death, and resurrection of Jesus the Christ.

There is neither time nor space enough to explore the relationship between East Afrikan/Egyptian cosmogony and West Afrikan cosmogonies. There are differences to be sure. There are also profound similarities. The complex notions of God that existed in the Afrikan consciousness prior to capture, enslavement, and colonization—prior to both the Islamic and Christian slave trades—were not completely erased by those traumatizing experiences. There remains within Afrikan peoples a deep and profound longing for re-union with God's Holy Spirit—the kind of re-union that erases the false dichotomy between sacred and secular, holy and profane seen and experienced in so much of 21st- century Christendom.

It is to the God-ideas of Afrika that leaders in the Afrikan Church in North America must return in order to fully grasp, internalize, and live out of the spiritual and covenantal commitments of our ancestors. This is a call to re-form the faith that is ours in God through the Christ. It is simultaneously the call to move beyond the spirit-defeating and spirit-destroying literalism of Christian fundamentalism. It is the third way—the way that leads to communion with the Afrikan God and to sharing in the paradise of God's eternal reigndom. Dr. Major J. Jones reminded us in his book *The Color of God: The Concept of God in Afro-American Thought,* "The 'new' of Christianity merely enlarged what was already authentic and foundational to the African God-concept in the mind of Africans who became the slaves of White Christians 300 and more years ago. The linkage between the African's concept of God and the Afro-American's concept of God must be seen against both the long-term religious traditions of African antiquity and the shorter-term religious traditions since slavery."[16]

These foundational commitments and engagements can and will, when implemented, transform the Afrikan psyche and enable us to manifest spirituality, individually and collectively, and that is liberating. They will also place us in opposition to the stultifying religious and political ideologies of empire. For example, embedded in the faith of our mothers and fathers is the divine feminine principle who complements her male counterpart in every conceivable way. Such a renewed vision of the Godhead will in time annihilate the destructive consequences of divine patriarchy. Yet those who choose a third way will simultaneously choose the way of the cross and crucifixion, death and ultimately, resurrection.

References

Budge, Sir E. A. W. (1959, 1987). *Egyptian religion.* Secaucus, NJ: Citadel Press.

Coleman, W. (2000). *Tribal talk: Black theology, herme-neutics, and African American ways of "telling the story."* University Park, PA: Pennsylvania State University Press.

Cross, J. (2003). God is a Negro, This far by faith: African-American spiritual journeys (Blackside and The Faith Project, in association with the Independent Television Service). PBS and ITVS. Retrieved from http://www.pbs.org/thisfarbyfaith/people/henry_mcneal_turner/html

Grant, J. (1989). *White women's Christ and Black women's Jesus: Feminist Christology and womanist response.* Academy Series AAR No. 64, edited by Susan Thistlethwaite. Atlanta: Scholars Press.

Greenberg, G. (1996). *The Bible myth: The African origins of the Jewish people.* Secaucus, NJ: Carol Publishing Group.

Hood, R. E. (1990). *Must God remain Greek? Afro cultures and God-talk.* Minneapolis, MN: Fortress Press.

Hopkins, D. N., & Cummings, G. (Eds.). (1991). *Cut loose your stammering tongue: Black theology in the slave narratives.* Maryknoll, NY: Orbis Books.

Jones, M. J. (1987). *The color of God: The concept of God in Afro-American thought.* Macon, GA: Mercer University Press.

Martin, T. (1976). *Race first: The ideological and organizational struggles of Marcus Garvey and the Universal Negro Improvement Association.* Westport, CT: Greenwood Press.

Walker, A. (1982). *The color purple.* New York: Harcourt Brace Jovanovich.

Williams, D. S. (1993). *Sisters in the wilderness: The challenge of womanist God-talk.* Maryknoll, NY: Orbis Books.

Young, J. U. (1990). *Black and African theologies: Siblings or distant cousins?* Maryknoll, NY: Orbis Books.

Chapter 5: Better Preparing Early Childhood Educators

By Dr. Charlyn Harper Browne

From the Head Start Reauthorization Act of 2007 to the Harlem Children's Zone that began in 1970, the goal of ensuring that young children are prepared to succeed in school has become a national priority. Although definitions and criteria of school readiness vary from state to state, findings from the National School Readiness Indicators Initiative (Rhode Island KIDS COUNT, 2005) identified a core set of common areas and indicators of school readiness: (a) ready children, (b) ready families, (c) ready communities, (d) ready services—health care and early education—and (e) ready schools.

One of the critical core indicators in the area of "ready services" involves early education teacher credentials.

> Early care and education programs . . . with highly qualified staff are more likely to produce positive outcomes for children's learning and development. Research shows that preschool teachers with at least a four-year degree and specialized training in early childhood are more effective and more actively engaged with the children they teach. (Rhode Island KIDS COUNT, 2005, p. 30)

One of the critical components in the area of "ready schools" involves understanding the role of culture in child development.

> Efforts to improve school readiness are most effective when they are responsive to and embrace the diverse cultural and language backgrounds

55

of families and children. . . . It is critical that the design and implementation of early childhood policies and practices be examined through a cultural lens. . . . The growing racial, ethnic, linguistic, and cultural diversity of young children requires that health, mental health, early childhood and education programs periodically reassess their appropriateness and effectiveness for the wide variety of families they serve. (Rhode Island KIDS COUNT, 2005, p. 39)

Preparing "Ready Early Childhood Educators"
Numerous researchers have concluded the quality of teachers is one of the most significant predictors of student success (Aaronson, Barrow, & Sanders, 2007; Chait, 2009; Chetty, Friedman, & Rockoff, 2011; Darling-Hammond, 2010; Nye, Konstantopoulos, & Hedges, 2004; Rockoff, 2004). Concerns about the impact of teacher quality on children's outcomes is further heightened by findings that show low quality teachers—defined as inexperienced, unqualified, out-of-field, ineffective teachers—are disproportionately distributed in schools located in communities plagued by persistent poverty and populated primarily by Black and Hispanic children (Chait, 2009; Clotfelter, Ladd, & Vigdor, 2005; Peske & Haycock, 2005).

Although the teacher equity clause in the No Child Left Behind Act of 2001 was an attempt in federal policy to address the inequitable distribution of high-quality teachers in high-resourced schools and low-quality teachers in low-resourced schools, the question of what constitutes "quality" still remains. Policymakers and education specialists tend to focus on increasing subject matter knowledge as a way improve teacher quality, but expertise in subject matter is not sufficient. Teachers also must have a high level of knowledge of current research in child development, with particular attention to early brain development. Furthermore, there is a need for teachers to move beyond simply trying to achieve cultural competence to developing an attitude of cultural humility (Tervalon & Murray-Garcia, 1988; Wear, 2008).

Knowledge of Early Brain Development, Social-Emotional Development, and Toxic Stress

> Apart from inquiry, apart from the praxis, individuals cannot be truly human. Knowledge emerges only through invention and reinvention, through the restless, impatient, continuing, hopeful inquiry human beings pursue in the world, with the world, and with each other (Freire, 2001, p. 71-72).

Perhaps the most important lesson I learned from Dr. Asa Grant Hilliard III was never to stop questioning, reading, reflecting, searching for meaning, and learning. Early childhood educators must heed this lesson as well if they are to be fully effective in guiding young children along a trajectory of healthy development, well-being, and academic success.

The need for early childhood educators to have more knowledge about child development is particularly important given the recent advances in the fields of neuroscience, pediatrics, and developmental psychology. Scientists in these fields have provided much evidence about the critical importance of: (a) understanding early brain development as the period in which the foundation for intellectual, social, emotional, and moral development is established; (b) providing experiences that promote social-emotional development in young children; and (c) understanding the impact of trauma on early brain development and addressing the needs of children who grow up in environments that create toxic stress (Munakata, Michaelson, Barker, & Chevalier, 2013; National Scientific Council on the Developing Child, 2005, 2007, 2010a, 2010b, 2012; Shonkoff, 2009; Shonkoff & Phillips, 2000; Thompson, 2001; Yeager & Yeager, 2013; Zelazo, Muller, Frye, & Marcovitch, 2003). When early childhood educators are grounded in the knowledge of early brain development, social-emotional development for young children, and the impact of toxic stress on development, they are much more effective in providing experiences that promote healthy development, well-being, and academic success and that mitigate risk factors which lead to poor outcomes.

Research has shown that young children's experiences at home and in early care and education settings shape the processes that determine whether their brains will have a strong or weak foundation for later learning, memory, logical reasoning, executive functioning, self-regulation, expressing emotions, socialization, and behavior control (Center on the Developing Child at Harvard University, 2010; Hawley, 2000; National Scientific Council on the Developing Child, 2004a, 2004b; Shonkoff, 2009; Shonkoff & Phillips, 2000). Early care and education environments prepare the developing brain to function optimally when they (a) provide proper nutrition and regularly scheduled periods of sleep and physical activity, and (b) consistently promote warm, nurturing, attentive social interactions. For example, a process called the "serve and return" interaction between young children and adults is critical for healthy brain development (Shonkoff). Serve and return occurs when young children solicit interaction through babbling, gestures, facial expressions, or focusing on an interesting

CHAPTER 5: BETTER PREPARING EARLY CHILDHOOD EDUCATORS
By Dr. Charlyn Harper Browne

object (the "serve"), and adults share and support the child's experience by responding in some manner (the "return"). The serve and return interaction helps to create neural connections in the young brain that build later cognitive and emotional skills (Shonkoff).

Conversely, lack of adequate nutrition, physical activity, appropriate sensory stimulation, child-adult interactions, or social-emotional developmental experiences disrupt early brain architecture and can have a decisively negative impact on future cognitive and social-emotional development (Center on the Developing Child at Harvard University, 2006; Grossman, Churchill, McKinney, Kodish, Otte, & Greenough, 2003; National Scientific Council on the Developing Child, 2007; Shonkoff, 2009). For example:

> Infants and children who are rarely spoken to, who are exposed to few toys, and who have little opportunity to explore and experiment with their environment may fail to fully develop the neural connections and pathways that facilitate later learning. Despite their normal genetic endowment, these children are at a significant intellectual disadvantage and are likely to require costly special education or other remedial services when they enter school. Fortunately, intervention programs that start working with children and their families at birth or even prenatally can help prevent this tragic loss of potential. (Hawley, 2000, p. 3)

More than learning to recite the alphabet and count, acquiring social-emotional competence is the primary developmental task of early childhood because it impacts all other developmental domains—physical growth, language development, and cognitive skills—and lays the foundation for later development (Brazelton & Sparrow, 2006; Brazelton & Greenspan, 2000; National Scientific Council on the Developing Child, 2004b).

> Sometimes called . . . infant mental health, healthy social and emotional development refers to a child's developing capacity to: (a) experience, manage and express the full range of positive and negative emotions; (b) develop close, satisfying relationships with other children and adults; and (c) actively explore their environment and learn. (Cohen, Onunaku, Clothier, & Poppe, 2005, p. 2)

Social-emotional development in young children does not evolve naturally; it is influenced by biological (e.g., the child's temperament), social (e.g., adult-child relationships), and environmental forces (e.g., child abuse or neglect) (Cohen, Onunaku, Clothier, & Poppe, 2005; Honig, 2002; Thompson, 2001). By providing consistent, affectionate, nurturing, sensitive, and responsive care, parents and other primary caregivers provide the conditions for children to develop a secure emotional attachment that contributes to healthy social-emotional development. In contrast, care that is inconsistent, unresponsive, or rejecting results in an insecure attachment that places young children at risk for developmental delays and mental health problems (National Scientific Council on the Developing Child, 2004b). National data support this assertion.

In a policy brief by Cooper, Masi, and Vick (2009), the National Center for Children in Poverty reported that unmet social-emotional developmental needs in early childhood can have negative effects later in life such as conduct problems, delinquency, and antisocial behaviors. Their data showed: (a) between 9.5% and 14.2% of children between 0-5 years old experience social-emotional problems; (b) approximately 9% of children who receive specialty mental health services in the United States are between 0-5 years old; and (c) almost 40% of 2-year-olds in early care and education settings had insecure attachment relationships with their mothers. Thus, there is increasing evidence that addressing social-emotional development should be a priority for early childhood educators, pediatricians, infant mental health providers, social workers, and others who work with young children and their families. This becomes an even greater imperative when serving vulnerable and highly stressed young children and their families given the potential for positive impact in many domains across the life span (Shonkoff & Phillips, 2000).

> During a "stranger-in-the-building" drill at an elementary school, I observed a group of 20 third-grade students who were instructed by their teacher to "get down on the floor and be quiet because somebody could be coming in here to kidnap you." One boy huddled alone, clinging to a leg of a table, trembling, and—by the look on his face—was in great distress. His two teachers ridiculed him for being "so scary" and laughingly said, "Boy, what's wrong with you? You know nobody is coming in here to get you."

Psychologists acknowledge that positive, manageable stressful situations (e.g., not being able to accomplish a task) are actually important for young children's healthy development. But when children experience prolonged, uninterrupted, overwhelmingly stressful events—that is, toxic stress—the result can be damaged, weakened systems and brain architecture that can have enduring effects (Center on the Developing Child at Harvard University, 2010, 2006). Toxic stress includes such experiences as child abuse, neglect, or abandonment; persistent fear; exposure to family or community violence; and betrayal by a trusted person or institution. Research has demonstrated that experiencing toxic stress during early childhood—without the buffering, protective relationships that help a child feel safe and secure—can (a) undermine the development of coping skills needed to address immediate and later-life challenges and adversities, and (b) establish the foundation for unhealthy lifestyles such as substance abuse and the perpetration of violence (Felitti et al., 1998; National Scientific Council on the Developing Child, 2010a, 2005).

How different the third grade boy's coping experience would have been had his teachers known about toxic stress and how to serve as a buffering, protecting agent for him. Rather than ridiculing him and asking, "What's wrong with you?" their responses and behavior would have been guided by the more sensitive and nurturing thought, "What has happened to you?"

Developing Cultural Humility
Given the increasing racial, ethnic, linguistic, and cultural diversity of the population in the United States, the need for those who serve young children and their families to develop a sense of cultural competence has long been emphasized. "Training in cultural competence has focused on teaching . . . concepts and practices of . . . racial and ethnic minorit[ies] . . . . The idea is if providers are more aware of the cultural background and beliefs of their clients, communication will be

easier" (California Health Advocates, 2007, p. 1). This type of training typically consists of teaching people "veritable laundry lists" (California Health Advocates) of names, ideas, traditions, and artifacts ostensibly characteristic of various racial, ethnic, or cultural "minority" groups. Although this type of training may be somewhat helpful, an implicit but erroneous assumption underlies not only this training but also the notion of developing cultural competence.

First, when the focus is on learning about *the other (minority) group's* culture, the assumption is that the majority group's culture is the norm. Thus, the minority group's culture is not simply conceived as *different* but represents *deviations* from the norm, and may ultimately be viewed as *deficiencies.*

In order for early childhood educators and others who serve racial, ethnic, linguistic, and culturally diverse young children and their families to be more effective and respectful, in addition to learning about culturally specific characteristics they must also conscientiously practice cultural humility. Cultural humility does not entail an examination of "the other group's" belief system. Rather, it entails active self-reflection and critical consciousness of one's own assumptions, beliefs, values, and worldview (California Health Advocates, 2007; Tervalon & Murray-Garcia, 1988; Wear, 2008). Cultural humility shifts the focus of understanding from other people to self-awareness.

> Cultural humility is an acknowledgement of one's own barriers to true intercultural understanding.... Knowing that one's own perspective is necessarily limited makes it much easier to be reflective and proactive in relation to one's prejudices and assumptions that may otherwise affect interactions with members of

a different culture. . . . Approaching each encounter with the knowledge that one's own perspective is full of assumptions and prejudices can help one to keep an open mind and remain respectful of the person seeking care. (Unite for Sight, 2013, http://www.uniteforsight.org/cultural-competency/module10)

Cultural humility can enable people to realize the error in assuming a single human norm so that differences no longer are presumed to be deviances and deficiencies. Furthermore, cultural humility can enable people to reflect on difficult topics such as "White privilege" and "internalized racism"; topics that if not addressed prevent productive self-reflection and effective interaction with others.

This chapter focused on early childhood educators' "readiness" as viewed through a cultural lens particular to the needs, aspirations, realities, and prospects of African American children. While government agencies, researchers, and nonprofit organizations have compiled regulations and data pertinent to the education of young children in the United States, there is an equally relevant and significant need for teachers to extend their efforts beyond, for example, knowledge of young children's early brain development and social-emotional development. Beyond the appreciation of the toxic stress that has been known to exist among more than a few families, beyond a teacher's ability to acquire cultural competence there is cultural humility—an acknowledgment that the continuous implementation of self-reflection and critical consciousness can bring about a kind of serve and return interaction which can enrich the readiness and engagement among early childhood educators. This kind of preparation and practice rewards the process and outcomes of teaching and learning.

References

Aaronson, D., Barrow, L., & Sanders, W. (2007). Teachers and student achievement in the Chicago public high schools. *Journal of Labor Economics, 25*(1), 95.

Brazelton, T. B., & Sparrow, J. D. (2006). *Touchpoints birth to 3: Your child's emotional and behavioral development.* Cambridge, MA: Da Capo Press.

Brazelton, T. B., & Greenspan, S. (2000). *The irreducible needs of children: What every child must have to grow, learn, and flourish.* Cambridge, MA: Perseus Books.

California Health Advocates. (April, 2007). *Are you practicing cultural humility? – The key to success in cultural competence.* Retrieved from http://www.cahealthadvocates.org/ news/disparities/2007/are-you.html

Center on the Developing Child at Harvard University. (2006). *Early exposure to toxic substances damages brain architecture.* Working Paper No. 4. Retrieved from http://www.developingchild.net/pubs/wp/Early_Exposure_Toxic_Substances_Brain_Architecture.pdf

Center on the Developing Child at Harvard University. (2010). *The foundations of lifelong health are built in early childhood.* Retrieved from http://www.developing child.harvard.edu

Center on the Developing Child at Harvard University (2011). *Building the brain's "air traffic control" system: How early experiences shape the development of executive function. Working Paper No. 11.* Retrieved from http://developingchild.harvard.edu/ index.php/resources/reports_and_working_papers/ working_papers/wp11/

Chait, R. (2009). *Ensuring effective teachers for all students: Six state strategies for attracting and retaining effective teachers in high-poverty and high-minority schools.* Washington, DC: Center for American Progress. Retrieved from http://www.american progress.org/wp-content/uploads/issues/2009/05/pdf/teacher_effectiveness.pdf

Chetty, R., Friedman, J. N., & Rockoff, J. E. (2011). *The long-term impacts of teachers: Teacher value-added and student outcomes in adulthood.* Cambridge, MA: National Bureau of Economic Research.

Clotfelter, C. T., Ladd, H. F., & Vigdor, J. (2005). Who teaches whom? Race and the distribution of novice teachers. *Economics of Education Review, 24*(4), 377.

Cohen, J., Onunaku, N., Clothier, S., & Poppe, J. (September, 2005). Helping young children succeed: Strategies to promote early childhood social and emotional development. *Early Childhood Research and Policy Report.* Washington, DC: National Conference of State Legislatures. Retrieved from http://main.zerotothree.org/site/DocServer/help_yng_child_succeed.pdf?docID=621

Cooper, J. L., Masi, R., & Vick, J. (August, 2009). *Social-emotional development in early childhood: What every policymaker should know.* New York, NY: National Center for Children in Poverty.

Darling-Hammond, L. (2010). *The flat world and education: How America's commitment to equity will determine our future.* New York: Teachers College Press.

Felitti, V. J., Anda, R. F., Nordenberg, D., Williamson, D. F., Spitz, A. M., Edwards, V. Koss, M. P., & Marks, J. S. (1998). Relationship of childhood abuse and household dysfunction to many of the leading causes of death in adults: The Adverse Childhood Experiences

(ACE) study. *American Journal of Preventive Medicine, 14*(4), 245-258.

Freire, P. (2001). *Pedagogy of the oppressed.* New York: Continuum.

Grossman, A.W., Churchill, J. D., McKinney, B.C., Kodish, I. M, Otte, S. L., & Greenough, W. T. (2003). Experience effects on brain development: Possible contributions to psychopathology. *Journal of Child Psychology and Psychiatry, 44,* 33-63.

Hawley, T. (2000). *Starting smart: How early experiences affect brain development.* Washington, DC: Ounce of Prevention Fund and ZERO TO THREE. Retrieved from http://www.ounceofprevention.org/news/pdf/Starting_Smart.pdf

Honig, A. S. (2002). *Secure relationships: Nurturing in-fant/toddler attachment in early care settings.* Washington, DC: National Association for the Education of Young Children.

Munakata, Y., Michaelson, L., Barker, J., & Chevalier, N. (2013). Executive functioning during infancy and childhood. *Encyclopedia on Early Childhood Development.* Retrieved from http://www.child-encyclopedia.com/ pages/PDF/cognitive-stimulation-executive-functions.pdf

National Scientific Council on the Developing Child. (2004a). *Young children develop in an environment of relationships.* Working Paper No. 1. Retrieved from http://www. developingchild.net

National Scientific Council on the Developing Child. (2004b). *Children's emotional development is built into the architecture of their brains.* Working Paper No. 2. Retrieved from http://developingchild.harvard.edu/index.php/resources/ reports and working papers/working papers/wp2/

National Scientific Council on the Developing Child. (2005). *Excessive stress disrupts the architecture of the developing brain.* Working Paper No. 3. Available at: http://developingchild.harvard.edu/library/reports_ and_working_papers/wp3/

National Scientific Council on the Developing Child. (2007). *The timing and quality of early experiences combine to shape brain architecture.* Working Paper No. 5. Available at: http://developingchild.harvard.edu/ library/reports_and_working_papers/wp5/

National Scientific Council on the Developing Child (2010a). *Persistent fear and anxiety can affect young children's learning and development. Working Paper No. 9.* Retrieved from http://developingchild.harvard.edu/ index.php/resources/reports_and_working_papers/ working_papers/wp9/

National Scientific Council on the Developing Child (2010b). *Early experiences can alter gene expression and affect long-term development. Working Paper No. 10.* http:// developingchild.harvard.edu/index.php/resources/ reports_and_working_papers/working_papers/wp10/

National Scientific Council on the Developing Child. (2012). *Establishing a level foundation for life: Mental health begins in early childhood. Working Paper 6.* Retrieved from http://developingchild.harvard.edu/index.php/ resources/reports_and_working_papers/working_ papers/wp6/

Nye, B., Konstantopoulos, S., & Hedges, L. V. (2004). How large are teacher effects? *Educational Evaluation and Policy Analysis, 26*(3), 237.

Peske, H., & Haycock, K. (2006). *Teaching inequality.* Washington, DC: The Education Trust.

Rockoff, J. E. (2004). The impact of individual teachers on student achievement: Evidence from panel data. *The American Economic Review, 94*(2), 247.

Rhode Island KIDS COUNT. (2005). *Getting ready: Find-ings from the National School Readiness Indicators Initiative, A 17 state partnership.* Retrieved from http://www.rikids.org/Matriarch/documents/Getting Ready – Full Report.pdf

Shonkoff, J. P. (2009). *Investment in early childhood develop-ment lays the foundation for a prosperous and sustain-able society.* Retrieved from http://www.child-encyclopedia.com/documents/Shonkoff ANGxp.pdf

Shonkoff, J., & Phillips, D. (Eds.) (2000). *From neurons to neighborhoods: The science of early childhood development.* Washington, DC: National Academy Press.

Tervalon, M., & Murray-Garcia, J. (1988). Cultural humil-ity vs. cultural competence: A critical distinction in defining physician training outcomes in multi-cultural education. *Journal of Health Care for the Poor and Underserved, 9*(2), 117.

Thompson, R. A. (2001). Development in the first years of life. *The Future of Children, 11*(1), 20-33.

Unite for Sight. (2013). *Module 10: Trust and Cultural Humility.* Retrieved from http://www.uniteforsight.org/cultural-competency/module10

Wear, D. (2008). On outcomes and humility. *Academic Medicine,* 83(7), 625-626. Retrieved from http://journals.lww.com/academicmedicine/Fulltext/2008/07000 /On_Outcomes_and_Humility.2.aspx

Yeager, M., & Yeager, M. (2013). *Executive function and child development.* New York: W. W. Norton.

Zelazo, P. D., Muller, U., Frye, D., & Marcovitch, S. (2003). The development of executive function in early childhood. *Monographs of the Society for Research in Child Development, 68*(3, Serial No. 274).

GYE NYAME

jeh N-yah-mee

Literally :

"EXCEPT GOD" OR
"TIS ONLY GOD"

Symbol of the omnipotence, omnipresence and immortality of God. "Except God, I fear none."

Proverb: *"Abodee santan yi firi tete; obi nte ase a onim n'ahyase, na obi ntena ase nkosi n'awie, gye Nyame."* *(This Great Panoroma of creation dates back to time immemorial, no one lives who saw its beginning and no one will live to see its end, Except God.)*

This symbol represents the mundane concept of the belief in the supremacy of God in the Ghanaian society. It refers principally to the greatness of God and it also reflects God's power over all of his creation.

Chapter 6: Gaining Credibility and Losing Knowledge, "We" and Cultural Validity: A Comparison of Child Development Associates 1.0 and 2.0

By Drs. Ernest Washington and James Young

> Professionals and laymen alike tend to be awed
> by data from assessment and procedural hocus
> pocus, and participate in the mystical delusion
> that all is well which appear crisp and ordered.
> Life itself is messy, uneven, approximate, and
> somewhat erratic, even when the figures make
> it appear otherwise. (Asa G. Hilliard III, 1973)

The transition from CDA 1.0 and 2.0 is a rare opportunity to compare perspectives, knowledge and validity in two related systems of assessing candidates in early childhood education. The new assessment system CDA 2.0 begins July, 2013. CDA 1.0, the older, Collaborative Approach to Evaluation, emphasized social support and collaboration, gradual mastery of the competencies, a constructivist view of knowledge, and implicit construct validity. In contrast CDA 2.0 is individual in its approach, norm-based, with a computer model of knowledge and an explicit focus on reliability and validity. Because CDA 2.0 is a statistical, computerized model, it is not surprising that the tools of reliability and validity are a natural fit and show the new system to its best advantage.

Once the transition is completed from the Collaborative Approach to Evaluation CDA 1.0 to the new norm-based CDA 2.0 evaluation system, practical knowledge will have lost prominence, and the "we" perspective and cultural validity will have disappeared. There is a connection between the reduced emphasis on practical knowledge, the "we" perspective, and cultural validity. The connection between these three ways of assessing competence is apparent only upon careful inspection, and then it is clear that something of significance and value was lost and not replaced. The purpose of this essay is to provide the background against which to compare CDA 1.0 and CDA 2.0, two systems for evaluating the process by which prospective educators focusing on early childhood attain certification.

Background on CDA
The original Collaborative Approach to Evaluation was based on practical knowledge of the Child Development Competency Goals and Functional Areas compiled and made available by Child Development Associates (CDA). This entity began in 1973, when the US Department of Health, Education, and Welfare's Administration on Children, Youth, and Families (ACYF) funded CDA's efforts to establish a credential that could formally and systematically improve the quality of early childhood education with training, testing, and direct observation of a candidate in a classroom environment. From 1975 on, CDA's credential for early childhood education became the only nationally recognized credential accepted throughout the US, valid for a set number of years and then renewable with further training, testing and observation.

In 1985, ACYF worked with the National Association for the Education of Young Children (NAEYC) in founding a separate, nonprofit entity to undertake the credentialing process. Since that time the Council for Early Childhood Professional Recognition (renamed the Council for Professional Recognition in 2003), has administered the training, testing and observation procedures and practices for early childhood educator-candidates. In 2012, the CDA Credential process began undertaking an update which includes, in addition to rolling out CDA 2.0, online applications and examinations created in conjunction with Pearson VUE and monitored at Pearson VUE's testing centers. Pearson VUE is a company in the Certification & Licensure Division of McGraw-Hill— a global multiconglomerate that specializes in, among other products and services, test development, data management and test centers in more than 150 countries.

Within this context and against this backdrop there is the development of CDA 1.0, its approach and widespread use, and the emergence of CDA 2.0 and its different approach and use and probable impact.

Three Ways of Assessing Competence and a New Perspective

Among the changes to note for CDA 2.0 and its norm-based approach to evaluation is that practical knowledge receded first. Practical knowledge involves knowing how to do things, solve problems, engage in activities, and play games with young children in the real world. In CDA 1.0 a candidate demonstrated mastery of these competencies in the classroom over an extended period of time. The collaborative approach was a competency basis in which the candidate could progress one step at a time, and not have to pass a summative, high-stakes examination. The candidate chose the what, when and how to demonstrate the competencies in concert with her support group, the assessment team. In CDA 2.0 there is a shift to tests that use theoretical knowledge as in the creation of a new norm-based test. This new evaluation system meets the standards of validity that center on factors of content and construct. In addition, the establishment of population validity, another component of CDA 2.0 is promising but not fully established.

The second way of assessing competence that was part of CDA 1.0 was the use of the "we" perspective. This perspective will disappear with the onset of CDA 2.0, along with its functional practice, the Community Assessment Team (CAT). The CAT was the mechanism of mentoring and support in CDA 1.0 and focused on the candidate's daily improvement and mastery of the competencies. Cultural validity, the third assessment method of CDA 1.0, was a primary aim of the collaborative approach. Every test instrument represents and encourages a point of view and values a particular form of knowledge. The new CDA does not purport to feature cultural validity—opting, instead, for a computer-focused model of validity.

What is new in this analysis is a perspective analysis of knowledge that is signaled by the pronouns "I," "he," "she" "it," and "we": 1) "I" an individual, subjective perspective, includes the knowledge of thinking, believing, feeling, and other subjective experiences to which only "I" or the candidate has access (Only I know what is going on in my head.); 2) an objective perspective that sees the world from an objective standpoint in which "he" and "she" acquire objective knowledge, perhaps about "it" by looking at the situation from the outside (Test constructors prefer a objective stance in which the candidate takes an outside perspective.); and 3) "we" is a group perspective in which participants share group knowledge about values, and ways of living, acting, and playing in community and culture.

The shift from "I" to "We", a shift in perspective, has been a major goal of the Collaborative Approach to Evaluation. The original conception of the CAE centered on an image of a low-income mom hesitantly climbing the educational ladder to make a better life for herself and her family. Her journey began at a local community center when she initiated the certification process that might take months or even years and was to result in her formally entering the profession of early childhood education. Toward that aim, a Community Assessment Team of supporters encouraged the candidate's development throughout the certification process as a teacher of increasing competence. In the beginning the candidate may have felt alone and uncertain, and may have blamed herself for lacking knowledge, confidence or other resources that could ease the process of certification. This is the "I" stage. In CDA 1.0 the Community Assessment Team used a supportive mode as the candidate improved her skills. The appearance of "we" in the team's dialogue was a signal of student progress and a means by which the candidate could change her perspective toward her efforts. This change in perspective had the additional, socializing effect of reinforcing the candidate's understanding that she was part of a culture/group involved in educating young children.

The lack of cultural validity in CDA 2.0 is a consequence of not emphasizing practical knowledge and the "we perspective" within the system. There is no instrument in CDA 2.0 from which to construct and support a cultural or group perspective. The collaborative approach encouraged and supported cultural traditions and ways of doing things. The community assessment team was created as a means of supporting the candidate within a culturally supportive community. Questions about culture and community do not have a place in the new assessment system.

Most importantly these two different approaches have different perspectives about what it is to be financially and educationally challenged, and to begin the climb of upward mobility by seeking to become a teacher. Once CDA 2.0 gets under way fully, the messiness of women of all cultures struggling to gain an educational foothold on the ladder of professional development no longer has an evaluative influence. The sense of agency gained from working collaboratively with a community member and advocate will disappear. The vision and structure involved in community control of the assessment process for early childhood educators will cease to exist in CDA 2.0. These issues will become nothing more than distractions from the main purpose of assessment. According to some commentators the new system with its built-in safeguards to ensure objectivity are an improvement over the imperfections of the collaborative approach to evaluation.

To many observers the change in the assessment system is a model of progress. One rather inefficient system is being replaced by a more efficient, scientific approach. To date (May, 2013) any knowledge that was lost or gained in transition has gone without official recognition or acknowledgment by CDA and Pearson. However, one of the aims of this essay is to clarify the different knowledge claims being made by CDA 1.0 and CDA 2.0, and not simply to mourn that which is no more or to celebrate that which is objective and new. The competing knowledge claims illuminate different aspects of human nature, and in the process support our assumptions about what it is to be a human being.

What knowledge was lost and gained in the transition between CDA 1.0 and 2.0? This essay answers that question by summarizing the two assessment systems' respective backgrounds, comparing practical and theoretical knowledge within the two systems and discussing a perspective analysis which reveals the social orientation of the systems. Then we will compare the two models using concepts of reliability and validity.

CDA 1.0: A Collaborative Approach to Evaluation
Reliability and validity are important issues in testing and assessment. The transition from CDA 1.0 to CDA 2.0 is a triumph of standardized testing over a collaborative approach to assessment. At its creation in 1973, CDA 1.0 was a bold innovation charting new directions in assessment. CDA 1.0

or the collaborative approach to evaluation began with a new series of assumptions about evaluation:

- the CDA candidate was a social and cultural human being,
- training and assessment were intertwined,
- the assessment process was collaborative rather than competitive, engaging the candidate in a gradual obtaining of competencies vs. an orientation toward tests, and the candidate compiled a portfolio of demonstrated competencies vs. the mere use of paper and pencils.

Implicit in CDA 1.0 was the fundamental assumption of collaboration, working together to help a candidate for certification achieve success.

This analysis retrofits a 40-year-old assessment system with 21st century research. The years have been theoretically kind and supportive of the system while its practices have led to its demise. No program of research was undertaken to examine and revise the system in its 40-year life span in which 300,000 candidates received certification (CDA, 2013).

Origins of a Collaborative Approach to Evaluation

The Collaborative Approach Process (CAP) which became CDA 1.0 was conceptualized by the Black Task Force in 1973, after a group of African American educators, psychologists and others met and developed a community-centered, culturally valid construct of evaluation for those pursuing the profession of early childhood education. One of the task force's members Stanley Crockett field-tested the pilot edition in 1974. Crockett was an African American educational psychologist who had been president of the Association of Black Psychologists (ABPsi) from 1970 to 1971 and was a leading proponent of improving evaluative measurements in education and social sciences. CDA 1.0 was conceived as a way of demonstrating the cultural strengths of African-American culture and to push back against racism in the social sciences. The educators and social scientists in the Black Task Force created an evaluation system in which collaboration was a goal and a sense of agency and control was in the hands of the CDA candidate. The Black Task Force did not accept the assumptions of positivism, IQ testing and "achievement" tests, or the prevailing assumptions about Black people. Positivism is the view that physics is the model, mathematics is the tool, and objectivity is the goal of social sciences. These anti-positivists refused to concede that physics was the model for the social sciences and emphatically rejected the prevailing use of tests and other measurements that attempted to define Black people.

Crockett (1973) defined collaboration as an emerging equality of attitude and behavior between two or more people organized around the achievement of a task. The minimum requirements for collaboration are: language usage that all can understand, the inclusion of all in the conversation, and equality of respect and collaboration. The CAP was initially conceived as an in-service educational training process in which there was an ongoing relationship between a child care center and the candidate.

The distinctive characteristics of the collaborative approach to evaluation are: (1) collaborative decision making through the community assessment team (CAT); (2) self-selection of the content, timing, and format of the evaluation by the CDA candidate; (3) development of an individual portfolio; (4) a 60-item test administered by an outside evaluator; and (5) the collaborative role of the evaluator or outside professional. This approach combines training and certification

in a continually monitored process. Today, as transition is
under way toward CDA 2.0 this strategy resembles a curriculum in which embedded tests are strategically placed in the
curriculum. As the CDA candidate attains certain competencies, progress is continually monitored and recorded. In CDA
1.0 this monitoring of the candidate was partly undertaken by
the CAT as an example of formative evaluation. In contrast,
the new CDA candidate will encounter summative evaluation. Today's high-stakes testing is an example of summative
evaluation in which there is one final score that tells the story.

Taking a Look at the Collaborative Approach

The collaborative approach process begins when the candidate and the director of the child care center work together in
choosing the individuals who make up the candidate's CAT.
Typically, a parent, a professional educator, the center director and the candidate are on the team. The professional
educator's major responsibility is to act as an advocate and
mentor for the CDA candidate. The purpose of the CAT is
fourfold. The team presents to the candidate a clear, under-
standable and acceptable statement of the skills to be learned.
Second, the explanation of these skills takes place in a group
context (CAT) that shares responsibility for facilitating the
candidate's professional growth and development. Third, the
team is responsible for collecting the necessary data to measure the candidate's progress in skills development. Fourth,
in shared decision making each member votes on the progress
of the candidate. The development of skills also known as
the candidate's training is a critical dimension of the CAP.

Self-selection is another critical dimension of the collaborative assessment process. The candidate chooses the timing (when), the format (how), the setting (where) and content
(what) of assessment. It also means the candidate maintains a

measure of control over his education and professional development. This strategy insures no two candidates will be assessed in exactly the same way.

An oral interview, initially a third component of the assessment process was designed to assess the candidate's theoretical knowledge of the competencies. Over the years the interview questions became too widely known and the security of the system was compromised so this component receded.

A portfolio is the fourth feature of the collaborative approach (called the Application), and data gathering was the method for the assessment of the CDA competencies. The original field-testing of the process indicated there should be multiple meetings of the CAT to create, define, and improve the development of the competencies. The then "new" technology of videotaping became the method for observing and monitoring the development of competencies. The emphasis has been on providing a balanced approach to data collection that includes video recordings, photographs, observations, anecdotal records, and interviews. Because the candidate controlled the tempo and format of the assessment process in CDA 1.0, the data collected has reflected the candidate's development of skills. Any data or content preferred by the candidate is grist for the data collection mill.

A fifth feature of the collaborative model (called a Verification Visit) involves the role of the outside evaluator or representative. The representative is an advocate for the outside evaluator, is a person approved by the CAT, and lends her expertise to enable the candidate to demonstrate her skills in the clearst, most reliable way possible.

The CDA website (2013) features the chart below that compares the steps undertaken by a candidate in CDA 1.0 and the steps undertaken in CDA 2.0.:

CHAPTER 6: GAINING CREDIBILITY AND LOSING KNOWLEDGE, "WE" AND CULTURAL VALIDITY...
By Drs. Ernest Washington and James Young

Comparison of the Current and Future CDA Credentialing Processes

Current CDA Credentialing Process

Step 1	2	3	4	5	6	
Anytime before application	Within five years before application	Within six months before application	Application	Within three months of Council approval of completed application	After Verification Visit	
■ Minimim of high school diploma/ GED or Enrolled in a high school vocational program	■ 120 hours of training in 8 subject areas ■ 480 hours of experience	■ Observation by CDA Advisor (Chosen by candidate ■ Professional Resource File (PRF) completed by Candidate ■ Parent Questionnaire (PG) gathered by Candidate	■ Candidate sends to the Council: -Application -Fee -Transcripts -and/or Certificates of training	■ Verification Visit conducted by Council Representative (assigned by Council): -Early Childhood -Studies Review exam Oral inteview -Review of PRF and PQs	■ Council Representative mails Verification Visit results to the Council	■ Council awards or denies Credential

"CDA 2.0" Credentialing Process (As of June 1, 2013)

Step 1	2	3	4	5	6	
Anytime before application	Within three years before application	Within six months before application	Application	Within 6 months of Council approval of completed application	After Verification Visit and CDA Exam	
■ Minimim of high school diploma/ GED or Enrolled in a high school vocational program ■ 120 hours of education in 8 Subject Areas	■ 480 hours of experience	■ Professional Portfolio (PP) completed by Candidate ■ Family Questionnaire (FQ) completed by Candidate	■ Candidate sends to the Council: -Application -Fee ■ Candidate receives approval that application is complete and the fee has been processed	■ Verification Visit conducted by CDA Professional Development Specialist (chosen by Candidate): -Review of PP, PQs, transcripts/ Certificates -Observation -Reflective Dialogue ■ Candidate takes CDA Exam at a local PearsonVUE testing center	■ Professional Development Specialist sends Verification Visit scores to the Council online ■ Pearson VUE sends exam scores to the Council online	■ Council awards or denies Credential

Origins of CDA 2.0

CDA 2.0 is a pristine example of best practices, educational technology, and a norm-based assessment system. Academic specialists developed test items based on the core competencies identified by Child Development Associates. Factor analytic studies demonstrated that the items in the test were measuring the different competencies. Two different tests, Forms A and B of CDA 2.0, are alternative tests for those individuals who may have to take the test more than once. Statistical analyses ensure that this test has reliability and content validity. Pearson VUE Company will administer the test to candidates in a standardized, monitored environment that ensures the security of the test. The use of alternative tests, reliability, face validity, and Pearson's testing procedures do not address the issue of construct or external validity.

The CDA 2.0 was created in part from the need to update and improve the system. CDA 1.0 had existed for almost 40 years. Since then, a great many aspects of early childhood education had changed or emerged, including understanding social-emotional development in young children, neuro-cognitive skills development, toxic stress and the presence of various media in a young child's home environment, to name a few. A reform of the system was necessary. The new system, CDA 2.0 consists of five components: the 65-item CDA Exam; the new Verification Visit based on the new R.O.R. protocol; a new kind of professional portfolio; a revised classroom observation; and a philosophical statement written by the candidate.

The professional portfolio is a professional development compilation in which the candidate reflects on her career. The portfolio includes (a) resources, (b) reflective statements on the competencies as guides, and (c) a professional philosophy statement that summarizes the candidate's learning experiences undertaken while compiling the portfolio. The resource collection includes evidence of knowledge of child abuse and neglect procedures for the state and mandatory reporting guidelines; certification of pediatric first aid training; copies of menus that the candidate has written to show knowledge of children's nutritional and special dietary needs; weekly lesson plans that include accommodations for those with special needs; the designs of one learning experience each, for science, language and literacy, creativity, fine motor skills, gross motor skills (an outdoor activity), self–concept building, emotional regulation, social skills, and math, all of which include the identification of materials, strategies, and goals needed for each learning experience. The portfolio should also include an appropriate bibliography of children's books.

Reflective statements of competence are a new component of the new assessment system. The candidate prepares written reflections on the teaching practices undertaken. Each statement should be 500 words in length. The reflections address CDA's specific competency goals such as *establish and maintain a safe, healthy learning environment*. The candidate is asked to write a reflective paragraph on for example, the sample menu included in the resource collection that the candidate participated in serving and/or designing. Another example of a written statement might reflect on the design of the room in which observations will occur and how this design influences learning. The same pattern of reflective writing is applied to the competency goals of 2) *to advance physical and intellectual competence,* 3) *to support social and emotional development and to provide positive guidance*, 4) *to establish positive and productive relationships with families, 5) to insure a well-run, purposeful program that is responsive to participant needs,* and 6) *to maintain a commitment to professionalism.*

The professional philosophy statement is the final reflective task for the candidate. She is asked to identify the personal values and beliefs around teaching and learning and describe her role as teacher in the lives of children and their families. This statement should be no longer than two pages. This is supplemented by the six to 12 pages of writing about her reflections on the competencies. A total of approximately a dozen pages of typed reflections are required of the successful candidate.

Clearly the successful candidate is someone with writing skills. Given the fact that CDA 2.0 is a norm-based assessment system, norms of what would be considered good-quality writing will contribute to the overall evaluation of the candidate's ability to be awarded or denied the credentials of an early childhood educator.

The observation of the candidate working with children, recording evidence relative to the competencies is a carryover from CDA 1.0. There is a new Comprehensive Scoring Instrument. The observations are structured to demonstrate the competence of the candidate.

The CDA exam comprises multiple-choice questions in 65 items. Five of the items include a photo and a short narrative, followed by a multiple-choice question about each scenario. One hour and forty-five minutes is allotted to complete the exam, which is available in English and Spanish. Pearson VUE Company administers the exam, insuring security and reliability of the testing process.

Comparing the Two Systems
The systems will be compared with regard to practical vs. theoretical knowledge, the social perspective (i.e., pronoun perspective), and the different forms of validity. The focus on practical knowledge and the community assessment team sets

CDA 1.0 apart from CDA 2.0 as well as other forms of assessment. The social perspective approach identifies the different knowledge systems valued by the respective systems. Tests are linguistic artifacts that inform us about the knowledge valued by institutions and stakeholders in power. By examining the different perspectives it is possible to compare the broad sweep of language knowledge with the more narrow focus of testing and assessment on their valued areas of knowledge.

Practical and Theoretical Knowledge and the Ghost in the Machine
CDA 1.0 and 2.0 differ in their emphasis on practical and theoretical knowledge. The collaborative approach to evaluation emphasized the acquisition of practical knowledge while 2.0 focuses on theoretical knowledge. Practical knowledge has to do with knowing how to do something while theoretical knowledge entails knowing that something is the case.

Intelligence is the ghost in the machine that purports to connect practical and theoretical knowledge according to the intellectualist legend. One of the tenets of the intellectualist legend is that muscular and physical movements are simple physical responses on the one side and mental abilities are on the other side. According to the legend intelligence is pulling the strings and connecting practical and theoretical knowledge. Intelligence by this account is superior and more important. The ghost connects the mental and the physical and diverts attention from practical and theoretical knowledge.

The exorcism of the ghost of intelligence is one of the projects taken on by Lev Vygotsky (1978). He pointed out that practical knowledge emerges when two or more individuals collaborate to solve a problem. Practical knowledge is created as students learn new skills in collaboration with

85

their teachers within a community of practice. Knowledge emerges as students are engaged in problem solving activities. The outcomes of active problem solving cannot be known in advance. The curriculum refers to the goals that are established in the beginning. With each new problem solving activity the teacher and student set new goals. The zone of proximal development is what a student can accomplish with the help of her teacher. Knowledge is not something that is transmitted from the heads of teachers to the heads of students. Instead, knowledge is created and recreated when teachers and students bring their previously learned experiences to the task of solving the problem.

Believing in a teacher is connected to practical knowledge. A student needs to believe in her teacher if she is to be a successful learner. Believing is more powerful than knowing because believing does not require evidence.

Theoretical knowledge refers to facts and theories about the world. Theoretical knowledge is justified true belief. (As in, I used to believe that there were people living on the moon; now I know there are no people on the moon because astronauts have been to the moon and found no one.) Theoretical knowledge emerges out of practical knowledge as collaborators search for and find the regularities and principles involved in solving problems. As time passes knowledge is codified and theoretical knowledge is separated from experience. The separation of practice and theory encourages the view that theoretical and practical knowledge belong to different realms, and a ghost in the machine connects the two.

The ghost in the machine merges into the shadows of practical and theoretical knowledge, reflections and writing skills. The shift to CDA 2.0, a computerized system facilitates the merger and signals to some that the ghost is pulling the strings in the background. In a world in which meritocracy

86

is the political rationale, intelligence is a mechanism that few question.

The collaborative approach with its emphasis on acquiring the practical knowledge to demonstrate competencies was a way of exorcising the ghost of measured intelligence. At the time of the creation of the collaborative approach there was a widely held assumption that people of color did not measure up intellectually.

CDA 1.0, CDA 2.0 and the Three Perspectives

According to the *Oxford Universal Dictionary on Historical Principles,* "perspective" comes from the Latin *perspectiva,* the science of optics. By the 1660s the definition of perspective had evolved to encompass a visible scene, viewpoint, or prospect. Today, perspective indicates one view amidst a number of different possible views. Perspectives are conceptual filters that highlight certain features in the social world. The three perspectives of "I," "he/she" or "it" and "we" highlight different parts of the social world.

"I," "she," "he," and "we" are pronouns that take the place of nouns. Third graders know this fact and also that nouns name people, places, and things. In CDA 1.0 "we" replaced nouns such as culture, collaboration, ethnicity, and community. "We" includes relationships and social knowledge of great value. CDA 2.0 makes little or no use of the concept of "we" and the spoken and unspoken knowledge that goes with it.

The perspectives of "I" (first person singular), "he," "she," or "it" (third person singular), and "we" (first person plural) are different ways of viewing the world. Empirical research in English, German, and French (Brunyé et al., 2009; Sato & Bergen, 2013) indicate pronouns are different perspectives for understanding the world. The choice of pronouns influences political decision making, in-group and out-group perceptions, attitudes toward justice, attitudes toward fairness, individual and collective thinking, aesthetic preferences, and forgiveness and vengeance.

Subjectivity and Empiricism

The first person perspective is subjective because it is based on experiences that only the knower possesses. The first person perspective is restricted to the thinking individual. This is true in particular about our conscious thought and feelings. Whatever consciousness may be, physically or otherwise, there is consensus that consciousness is only accessible to privileged first person access. It is obvious that my access to my thoughts and feelings is different from your access to those same thoughts and feelings. I have firsthand experiences with my pain while you can only infer my pain from my behavior. A first person perspective is important because it reveals how the individual thinks, feels, believes and seems herself. Only "I" can tell you about my sense of self.

The second person single perspective is intersubjective because it is a relation between two thinking beings. It is also the origins and beginnings of imagination. This perspective depends on the ability of one individual to read the mind of another; this is an act of imagination. A second person perspective involves drawing on one's own experience in order to imagine the mental states of another sentient being. Taking this perspective does provide a payoff. The second person perspective is a unique access to certain facts, namely other persons' mental states in a social context. Reading others' minds is so fundamental to being a person that it is difficult to tease it out of a conversation. It is only when it is not present as in those on the autism spectrum that its value is evident. (The second person singular, "you" fills the space left by "I" by imagining other possibilities for persons, things, and situations.) This analysis will not focus on the second person singular "you," or the other forms, but will focus on the perspectives of "I," "he," "she," "it" and" "we."

The third person single perspective includes non-privileged access to all kinds of individuals and objects. Scientific research is the premier example of a third person perspective. Empiricism or experimental evidence is based on pubic observation gathered in accord with certain agreed upon rules. Almost anything can be observed using a third person perspective. The third person applies to the physical, social and the subjective, and this is why it has been called "objective."

The first person plural perspective "we" is an entrée to group knowledge. Membership in groups is an irreducible necessity for our understanding and explanations of the social world. Groups are composed of individuals who share a commitment to certain goals, intentions, attitudes, or actions, and share common knowledge. Knowing participation in the practices or language games of a group is the equivalent of the constitution of the group. The commitment of these individuals is as a unit or a whole. This commitment is made with individuals sharing common knowledge, beliefs, desires, intentions, and goals that together constitute "we."

Pronouns and Assessments: A Review of the Literature
Changing pronouns changes perspectives on the world. Beginning in childhood the use of pronouns proceeds in a developmental pattern. Lewis and Ramsey (2004) examined the relation of visual self-recognition, first person singular pronoun use and pretend play. Children showing self-recognition used more personal pronouns and demonstrated more advanced pretend play than did children not showing self-recognition. Third person singular pronouns appear in response

to what, when, where and how questions, and are influenced by early language development and the preceding discourse (Campbell, Brooks, Tomasello, 2000).

Changes in pronouns are an indicator of psychotherapeutic change in personality disorders. Arntz, Hawke, Bamelis, Spinhoven and Molendijk (2012) found that the self-view in personality disorders changes over the course of therapy. With the use of first person pronouns, negative emotions declined significantly while the use of present tense verbs and positive emotions increased as a result of therapy. Seider, Hirschberger, Nelson, and Levenson (2009), examined the relationship of personal pronouns "I" and "we" and marital satisfaction. The greater use of "we" was associated with desirable qualities of interaction, lower arousal, and less negative emotions.

Changing linguistic perspectives has been found to be helpful in treating trauma. Writing about trauma from a third person perspective facilitated greater benefits and longer lasting effects and fewer days lost to illness. These data suggest it is beneficial to use third person in writing about traumatic events (Andersson and Conley, 2012).

Khawaja, Chen and Marcus (2012) transcribed the speech of bush firefighters as they went about their work. With high loads of work, people spoke more and used longer sentences, disagreed more often with team members, and there was more use of plural pronouns and decreased use of personal pronouns.

The non-normal use of pronouns has been associated with a variety of pathological conditions. Schizophrenics use more second person pronouns and they have an abnormality in interpersonal relationships; they do not make distinctions between concepts being self-generated or from somewhere else. Hobson, Lee, and Hobson (2010) found that participants with autism were less likely to use third person pronouns or to show patterns of eye gaze reflecting engagement with an interloculator's stance vis-à-vis a third person. In these settings, atypical third person pronoun usage seemed to reflect limited communicative engagement but first person pronouns were relatively spared.

Na and Choi (2009) found that repeated exposures to the first person singular pronoun "I" activates an individualist orientation while first person plural pronouns activate a collective orientation. Each perspective affords access to different forms of knowledge. The first person perspective offers privileged access to the subjective world that only the individual knows. The second person singular perspective offers access to the minds of others through imagining the minds of others. The third person singular with its use of "he," "she" or "it" accesses observations that can be checked for objectivity and evidence. The first person plural "we," offers access to the group, identity, social thought and the behavior of others.

This very brief review of the literature affirms that a shift in social perspectives is signaled by a shift in pronouns. This suggests that as candidates move through the assessment process there is shift from an "I" to a "we" perspective. This informs us about the development of the candidate, a neglected aspect of CDA 2.0.

Validity Framework

The components of the two systems are "stand-alone" instruments that can be evaluated separately. Each of the components contributes to the prediction of success for the candidate. (One can imagine a regression equation in which each independent variable contributes to the prediction of the dependent variable or success as a teacher.) The usefulness of any test is a function of whether it is reliable and valid. Of course, reliability is required if a test is to be valid. This conceptual analysis will examine four different forms of validity: construct validity, cultural validity, ecological validity, and population validity.

Construct validity is the most fundamental of the validity issues because it is based on the assumption that population, ecological, and interpretive validity have been included in the logic of inquiry. The establishment of construct validity begins with the unraveling of the effects of constructs from the effects of methodology. In practical terms this means examining a construct from three or more methodological points of view. For example, it is possible to make judgments of courage through observation, testing, and interviewing. The intersection of the methodologies points toward the key variables in the construct of courage.

Cultural validity hinges on the premise that human actions are teleological or goal directed. Action is guided by rules that regulate conduct, practices, and institutions. The basis for teleology is the individual making choices about goals and how to achieve them. The intentional nature of human action places the individual at the center of the explanation of action. It is the individual who is best able to describe the motivational background, the goals and means to achieve the goals which set the stage for actions. The question of whether to utilize the words, motives, and purposes of the informants or the interpretations of social scientists is one of the critical methodological questions in social science research. This dispute goes back to Franz Boas and Leslie A. White in the early 20th century. Boas and those that agreed with him contended that each group has to be understood on its own terms and that it is the actor's interpretation of phenomenon which forms the basic datum of the discipline. White and his supporters are advocates of a scientific approach in which causal explanation is used to search for "universal" dimensions of culture.

Ecological validity is concerned with the linkages between the complexities of any population and their respective adaptations. Sub-populations adapt to different environment niches and thus make generalizations difficult. Ecological validity has been defined by Bronfenbrenner (1977) as the extent to which the environment experienced by the subject has the properties it is assumed to have by the experimenter. He defines the ecology of human development as the scientific study of the progressive, mutual accommodation throughout the life span between a growing human organism and the changing immediate environments in which the organism lives, as this process is affected by relations obtaining within and between immediate settings as well as the larger social context, both formal and informal in which settings are embedded.

Population validity has been approached traditionally by distinguishing the population on which an instrument is normed and the population to which it is applied. Two different tiers of assumptions are being made. The first set of assumptions has to do with generalizations from the population on which the test is normed to the individuals being assessed. A second level of assumptions about generalizations is namely that a generalization or norm of behavior holds true or is valid for two different populations.

Perceiving the Approaches of CDA 1.0 and 2.0
Social perspective and validity is the lens through which to examine CDA 1.0 and 2.0. The social perspective approach fits the Collaborative Approach and the validity approach fits the new norm-based approach to assessment. The powerful

strength of the computer/objective model of knowledge is that it can include the other forms of knowledge. It is possible to objectify the subjective experiences that only "I" possess. This is behaviorism. For example, I observe the expression on your face, the way your voice quivers, and the manner in which you hold your body. This is behaviorism, and it should not be forgotten that behaviorism dominated psychology for 50 years. It should not be forgotten that behaviorism falters when it attempts to give meaning to experiences. The problem of meaning is a vexing and difficult issue for behaviorism.

What's Ahead: CD 3.0?
The biggest changes in the system will be the expansion of the competences to include imagination, creativitiy, and character.[1] Here is an opening in assessments of the future for the inclusion of "you" and imagining other minds and things. Meanwhile, there is little to contradict the likelihood that assessment will continue to feature greater emphasis on writing skills, extensive portfolio contents, and data management and a network of monitored, standardized testing centers through CDA's contracts with companies like Pearson.

Summary
This chapter has focused on one of Asa Hilliard's commitments, the safeguarding of a collaborative, community-centered approach to evaluating those who would become early childhood educators. While this approach had been in effect via concomitant effort from organizations such as ABPsi and the Black Task Force, comprising a major influence in the formation of CDA 1.0 in the early 1970s, over time this assessment system needed an overhaul and upgrade. However, the new version of assessment, CDA 2.0 will become a distinctly different approach and have a contrasting perspective

toward candidates for early childhood education careers. Practical knowledge, a feature of CDA 1.0 will lose prominence in CDA 2.0 as will the "we" perspective embedded in CDA 1.0's assessment team of support for candidates; cultural validity will recede and be replaced by a norm-based, statistical, computerized model of validity and reliability. A review of some of the literature surrounding these issues indicated that the change in perspective—from "I" and "we" to "he," she," and it"—benefits an objective, norm-based approach to evaluation and reflects a change in how a system's organizers and managers approach the notion of assessing and validating people's efforts to improve their involvement in educating young children.

We will not get to discover how Brother Asa G. Hilliard III would weigh in as CDA 2.0 gets fully under way and thousands of candidates experience this assessment process; however, we have the methodology and the expertise to facilitate our own critical inquiries. We can use Hilliard's appreciation for implementing collaborative approaches to evaluating teachers- and teaching-in-progress—as well as the founding years and persons of the Collaborative Approach to Evaluation—as a means and a guiding force for the continual process of vigilance and re-control of our own assessment of early childhood educators.

References

Andersson, M. A., & Conley, C. S. (February, 2013). Optimizing the perceived benefits and health outcomes of writing about traumatic events. *Stress and Health, 29*(1), 40-49.

Arntz, A., Hawke, L. D., Bamelis, L., Spinhoven, P., & Molenijk, M. L. (March, 2012). Changes in natural language use as an indicator of psychotherapeutic change in personality disorders. *Behavioural Research Therapy, 50*(3), 191-202. doi: 10.1016/j.brat2011.12.007

Bronfenbrenner, U. (July, 1977). Toward an experimental ecology of human development. *American Psychologist, 32*(7), 513-531.

Brunyé, T., et al. (2009). When you and I share perspectives: Pronouns modulate perspective taking during narrative comprehension. *Psychological Science, 29*(1), 27-32. Retrieved from http://ase.tufts.edu/psychology/spacelab/pubs/Brunye_etal_psychsci.pdf

Campbell, A., Brooks, P., & Tomasello, M. (December, 2000). Factors affecting young children's use of pronouns as referring expressions. *Journal of Speech, Language, and Hearing Research, 43*(6), 1337-1349.

CDA Council. Comparison of the current and future CDA Credentialing Processes. Retrieved from http://www.cdacouncil.org/storage/documents/Comparison_Chart_jan_2013.pdf

Child Development Associates (2013). What is a CDA? Retrieved from http://easycda.com

Crockett, S. (Winter, 1973). The role of the researcher in education settings: Perspectives on research and evaluation. *Journal of Social Sciences, 29*(1), 81-85. doi: 10.1111/j.1540-4560.1973.tb00062.x

Hilliard, A. G. (1973). *The intellectual strengths of Black
children and adolescents: A challenge to pseudo
science.* New York: Institute of Afrikan Research.

Hilliard, A. G. (Ed.). (1991). *Testing African American stu-
dents.* Special re-issue of *The Negro Educational
Review, 38*(3), April-July, 1987. Morristown, NJ:
Aaron Press.

Hobson, R. P., Lee, A., & Hobson, J. A. (2010). Personal
pronouns and communicative engagement in autism.
*Journal of Autism and Developmental Disorders,
40*(6), 653-664. doi: 10.1007/s10803-009-0910-5

Khawaja, M. A., Chen, F., & Marcus, N. (August, 2012).
Analysis of collaborative communication for linguistic cues of cognitive load. *Human Factors, 54*(4),
518-529.

Lewis, M., & Ramsey, D. (December, 2004). Development
of self-recognition, personal pronoun use and pretend play during the second year. *Child Development, 75*(6), 1821-1831.

Murray, J. A. H. (Ed.). (1937). *Oxford universal dictionary
on historical principles.* New York: Oxford University Press.

Na, J., & Choi, I. (November, 2009). Culture and first-person
pronouns. *Personality and Psychology Bulletin,
35*(11), 1492-1499. doi. 10.1177/0146167209343810

Sato, M., & Bergen, B. K. (2013). The case of the missing
pronouns: Does mentally simulated perspective play
a functional role in the comprehension of person?
Cognition, 127. Retrieved from http://www.cogsci.
ucsd.edu/~bkbergen/papers/SatoBergen2013.pdf

Seider, B. H., Hirschberger, G., Nelson, K. L., & Levenson,
R. W. (September, 2009). We can work it out: Age
differences in relational pronouns, physiology, and

behavior in marital conflict. *Psychology and Aging, 24*(3), 604-613. doi: 10.1037/a0016950

Vygotsky, L., & Cole, M. (1978). *Mind and society: The development of higher psychological processes.* Cambridge, MA: Harvard University Press.

Williams, R. L. (August, 2008). A 40-year history of the Association of Black Psychologists (ABPsi). *Journal of Black Psychology, 34*(3), 249-260.

Chapter 7: "Are We Asking the Right Question?" Reflections on Asa Hilliard and the Notion of Objectivity in Research

By Sarita K. Davis, PhD, MSW

When addressing a controversial issue facing African-descended people, Asa Hilliard would often begin the conversation with the following probe: "Are we asking the right question?" In my budding days as a social worker and evaluator I struggled to wrap my mind around his seemingly curious response to much of what has constituted research on African people. I would say, to myself of course since at the time I was not involved in research with him, "Asa, the data are clear. Our standardized test scores are lower. Our health disparities are greater. African-descended people are an at-risk culture!" During this imaginary dialogue I anticipated the probable response from Asa, something like, "Data are not objective." Over time I came to understand exactly what Asa meant. The greatest myth perpetuated by Western research is that research is objective. Consequently, if Western research is objective, its processes must be fair, its questions must be just, and of course its conclusions must be correct.

The epistemology underlying any research framework is critical to the inquiry process as it carries the validity of the research question, the assumptions of the inquirer, the framing of the investigative process, the interpretation of the findings and the implications for the community (Carruthers, 1996; Dixon, 1971; Dixon, 1976; Hilliard, 1992; Kershaw, 2003). While other ways of knowing are growing in social science research, positivism is still considered the gold standard

(Carruthers, 1996; Smith, 2002). Consequently, it is important that we interrogate claims of objectivity to ensure that they are not positivist practices dressed up in post-positivist clothing.

Today, research exists in an era when "cultural competence" is being touted as a *necessary* response to improve research with historically marginalized groups; very little attention has been given to the application of African-centered research frameworks as a process for formulating and constructing research that affects African-descended people. In this chapter, I will attempt to illustrate how Asa's insightful probe strikes at the Achilles heel of Western research and its false pronouncements of objectivity. In this exploration of objectivity in research I discuss where, why, and how bias is woven into the fab-ric of Western research. In so doing, I draw upon Elaine Pinderhughes's power theory to explore the relationship between the researcher and the object of her work. Additionally, I attempt to illustrate how issues relevant to bias in this context can be mediated. The subsequent discussion explores the topic in four sections: 1) Research Problem Formulation; 2) The Philosophy of Social Science Research; 3) The Practice of Research; and 4) Democratizing Research. By understanding the roots and branches of social science research the reader should understand how bias is embedded in the research process as well as how to mediate differentials.

Research Problem Formulation

How do researchers come up with ideas for research projects? While there is no singular answer, three primary sources are constant—practical problems, the literature, and culture. Some

CHAPTER 7: "ARE WE ASKING THE RIGHT QUESTION?"...
By Sarita K. Davis, PhD, MSW

researchers are involved with human service delivery and research projects evolve out of the needs in their field. Other researchers are not directly involved in service delivery but are charged with quality assurance. For example, my sister has worked for a major airline carrier as a ticket agent so I offer the scenario of ticket counter personnel and back injuries as an example of field-related research. Ticket agents and skycaps lift a lot of luggage and packages in their jobs, especially on international flights. Consequently, if five or 10 out of every 100 ticket agents strained their backs on average over the period of one year, the costs would be enormous. Even minor injuries could result in increased absenteeism. Major ones could result in lost jobs and expensive medical bills. The airline industry figures that this is a problem that costs tens of millions of dollars annually in increased health care. The airline industry has developed a number of approaches, many of them educational, to try to reduce the scope and cost of the problem. As a result, many of these practical problems that arise in practice can lead to extensive research efforts.

Another source of research topics is the literature in a specific field. Oftentimes researchers get ideas from the gaps found and recommendations made in existing studies. This process of engaging in research by linking existing research with new people, places, and times serves to build the knowledge base in ways that cut across disciplines, practices, and theoretical orientation. This approach is standard practice in academia, government, and the sciences.

Finally, and probably most importantly, some researchers just think up research problems on their own. Let's be clear, researchers do not live in a vacuum so their ideas are influenced by the world in which they live—background, culture, education, class, etc.

In summary, social science research questions generally evolve out of a context, be it professional or personal experience, practice, or a discipline. Despite the historical claims that research is objective, we see that the process of research problem formulation oftentimes is informed by a situation, incident, dialogue, etc. As these frameworks are all guided by interpretation of the receiver, it is safe to assume that research questions come from a place that is informed by value positions. This finding begs the questions: Whose values are (or are not) being considered? How do these values influence the research question?

The Philosophy of Social Science Research

Contemporary research is rooted in philosophy and logical reasoning. In the past, philosophers and scientists were primarily concerned with trying to understand the world around them, thereby generating knowledge and truth. Epistemology is the philosophy of knowledge or how we come to know. The assumption that early philosophers and scientists made in laying the foundation of research was that there was a single objective reality. Of course, nobody really knows how we can best interpret the world around us, but by understanding the epistemological debate at the core of research we gain insight as to how the notion of power is introduced in the research context. While the epistemological schools of thought undergirding social science research have grown over the years, they all can be placed under one of the following two broad categories: positivism and post-positivism.

The positivist believes that the purpose of science is simply to observe, measure, and report what is seen. A positivist would argue that knowledge (truth) beyond what can be observed is impossible. Because we cannot directly observe feelings, thoughts, perceptions, etc., positivists believe that behavior is the only legitimate source of knowledge. Disciplines that embrace positivism include: medicine, public health, biology, anthropology, and some branches of education and psychology.

However, the post-positivist believes that there is a reality independent of our thinking about it and it can be studied. The post-positivist asserts that all measurement is fallible, so high importance is placed on multiple measures and observations as a way to reduce error and get a better handle on what's happening in reality. The most important belief of the post-positivist is that all observations are theory-laden and that scientists are inherently biased by their cultural experiences, worldviews, and so on. Some of the other theories that fit under the umbrella of post-positivism include: relativism, hermeneutics, constructivism, and feminism. The emergent theories generally agree that there are multiple realities based on consciousness, gender, and experience. Some differ, however, as to whether our realities can be mutually understood or even reconciled. Disciplines that lean in the direction of post-positivism include: sociology, nursing, history, and social work. Please note that these categories are not ironclad. Some disciplines, like education and psychology, take shelter in both schools of thought.

At the end of the day, the primary differences between the positivist and post-positivist are found in the notion of a singular reality (truth) and the objectivity of the researcher. With the epistemological sheets pulled back so to speak, we can begin to see how power sleeps in the bed of research. Based on our understanding of epistemology and its role in research, we see that bias is embedded in the very fabric of a discipline or field of study.

Most researchers are socialized in the values and practices of their discipline in their academic education and professional development. Gatekeepers such as faculty, staff, licensing bodies, professional affiliations, etc., indoctrinate researchers in the history, goals, practices, and expectations of their chosen field. As we learned earlier, most disciplines clearly fall under one of the two primary epistemological schools of thought. As a result, some disciplines inherently regard the values, beliefs, customs, and practices of a community as "barriers" to research while others embrace them as opportunities to engage in self-determination, decolonization, and social justice (Smith, 2002). Scholars and researchers have noted that the lack of critical reflection about one's field can create a schism or bifurcation within the researcher, especially if the researcher is a member of a marginalized group. Patricia Hill Collins (1991) refers to this disconnect as "the outsider within" positioning of research. For example, if you are a Black female social worker and researcher raised in South Central Los Angeles (like me), you probably have some understanding of or proximity to oppression based on race, class and gender inequities and its effect on the sexual decision making among Black women. However, your education and training suggest that neither your personal experience nor the social and historical context of Black women's relationship with their bodies is relevant to the landscape of your practice. This predicament is not uncommon for a great many Black researchers. They struggle to engage the disconnections that are apparent between the demands of their own research with the realities encountered in working with other marginalized communities with whom they share lifelong relationships.

In summary, for the researcher the primary allure of scientific inquiry is providing information that fills a gap in

knowledge. So whether the researcher is a positivist and believes in an objective truth or the researcher is a post-positivist and believes she is providing the best possible fallible answer available at the moment—both are vulnerable to the
powerful high produced from knowing. We also learned that
contrary to widely held beliefs about the "objectivity" of science, we know that research questions are not formed in a
vacuum and are value-laden propositions which are reinforced
through disciplinary training, education, and professional
development—and which may be more acutely felt by researchers who identify with marginalized populations. As a
result, we see that researchers encounter issues related to
power regardless of their epistemological stance or social location. This reality is foundational if we are to understand
Asa's probe: "Are we asking the right question?" Disciplinary ideology is the basis for how knowledge is constructed
and subsequently how we identify and frame the research
question. The following section explores how power shows
up in the practice of research.

The Practice of Research
This section details where and how power manifests in the
process of conducting research. In so doing, I will define the
five broad stages of the research cycle and discuss how power
manifests itself at each stage. At the end of this discussion
the reader should understand how social scientists invite biases into the research process through Westernized thinking
and the use of colonized methods.
*So how do issues related to bias show up in the research
cycle?* The social science research cycle occurs in the following five sequential stages: 1) Problem/Opportunity Identification; 2) Purpose; 3) Conceptualization; 4) Implementation;
and 5) Interpretation.

Problem/Opportunity Identification

In the Problem/Opportunity Identification stage, the individual or entity that frames the research is exercising power. The notion of a "Problem" is typically how research begins. A colleague added the term "Opportunity" to this phrase several years ago because she felt defining everything as a problem was pathological. I agreed with her insight and continue to incorporate this term in my approach to research. This thinking supports Pindherhughes's "one-up, one-down" scenario in the power theory (1983). Applied to research this notion occurs when those who are the focus of the research are vulnerable; they may become the pitiful objects of the benevolent researcher, an overly sympathetic segment of society that improves its functioning at the expense of the "pitiful." As a result, the researched become a vulnerable population, chronically impaired by the very attention designed to help. No matter how good the principle behind such research, it is essentially impossible to implement without the built-in complications of the projection process. Pinderhughes goes on to say that this dynamic can keep the victim, or research group, in relatively powerless positions where they serve as a balancing mechanism for the systems in which they exist.

Purpose

In the Purpose stage the goals, aims, and benefits of the research are explained.

Where bias shows up:

A majority of research is formulated, designed, and executed without the input of the researched. This practice creates another imbalance by placing the researched in a purely reactive situation. They are unable to exercise initiative, set goals, make choices, plan, exercise initiative or assume leadership (Pinderhughes, 1983). Consequently, one fails to create a sense of mastery over life (Aponte, 1994). I will explore more innovative approaches to research that attempt to remedy this imbalance in the final section.

Another dynamic at this stage has implications for the researcher. Pinderhughes says that the result of having a position of power includes being controlling and/or dominating, expressing arrogance and displaying paranoia which result from delusions of superiority, grandiosity, and an unrealistic sense of entitlement. The outcome may be having distorted perceptions and being unable to realistically assess one's own reality and that of the powerless. So in applying Pinderhughes's power theory to the research context, the pure gratification of having this type of power may encourage researchers to isolate and distance themselves from the researched, which in turn can result in a comfort with sameness and an intolerance of differences. Moreover, having power can create or satisfy a psychological need to have a victim, someone to scapegoat and control in order to maintain one's equilibrium.

Conceptualization and Implementation
Conceptualization is the stage of the research process where the project is detailed, including the sample, design, measurement, and data analysis. Implementation is where the research is executed. As they function together as idea and plan, I will discuss them here jointly.

Where power shows up:
I think the second most critical appearance of power in research occurs at the juncture of conceptualization and implementation. It is an interactive level characterized by dominance-subordinance or equality. Ultimately, this is the location at which researchers decide the roles to be played by themselves and the researched, and the value of each. These choices have implications for all stakeholders on multiple levels.

A controversial example of the long-term conse-quences of the dominance-subordinance stance can be found in the Moynihan Report. In March 1965, a young sociologist and political appointee in the US Labor Department named Daniel Patrick Moynihan wrote a report "The Negro Family: The Case for National Action," warning of high levels of out-of-wedlock births in the Black community. Interestingly, the report was intended as an internal document but was leaked to sources outside of the government. The report noted that nearly a quarter of all Black children were born out of wed-lock, a ratio that had been rising since the end of World War II. Such a trend, Moynihan warned, could deepen Black pov-erty rates and lead to a "tangle of pathologies." While the Moynihan Report acknowledged structural factors such as slavery and growing urbanization of the Black community it is remembered more for its criticism of Black mothers and absentee fathers. In Linda Smith's book *Decolonizing Meth-ods and Indigenous Research* (2002) she shines a bright spot-light on the problem of outsiders framing and interpreting the observations of indigenous (insider) culture. She says, "Trav-ellers' stories were generally the experiences and observa-tions of white men whose interactions with indigenous 'soci-eties' or 'peoples' were constructed around their own cultural views of gender and sexuality. . . . [These views were] based on Western notions of culture, religion, race and class" (p. 8). Once popularized these perspectives appeal not only to voy-eur, soldier, romantic, and enlightened scholar but also the powerless oppressed who begin to internalize the travelers' tales as facts.

Smith (2002) attributes this "insider/outsider" polar-ization to the fact that most researchers, even those of color, are primarily trained within Western academies and use those disciplinary practices. Even indigenous researchers, such as those trained in the ways of knowing of tribal communities, struggle against socially imposed ways of knowing. Many indigenous researchers individually have great difficulty engaging with the apparent disconnections between the demands of research and the realities they encounter among their own indigenous communities and others with whom they share lifelong relationships.

A number of ethical, cultural, political, and personal issues can present special difficulties for indigenous researchers who in their own communities partially work as insiders; are often employed for this purpose; and may work across clan, ethnic, linguistic, age, and gender boundaries. They simultaneously work within their research projects and institutions as (a) insiders within a particular paradigm or research model, and (b) outsiders because they are often marginalized and perceived to represent an African or rival interest group. Collins (1991) refers to this positioning of research as "the outsider within." This relationship can depict the dominant path of outsider-imposed constructs, such as government, research, and media, as opposed to the socially constructed ways of knowing that emerge from within the community, including folk art, music, and stories.

Cultural relevance and the identity and social location of the researcher have been debated for more than two decades. Hood (1998, 2001) argues that researchers of color are more able to bridge the gap among cultural nuances because of their shared understanding of African realities. Madison (1992) goes further in saying that researchers who have minimal contact with other African groups, regardless of ethnicity, may not be the most suitable to decide whether a particular intervention is appropriate for meeting their needs. Ultimately, the insider/outsider dilemma must be taken seriously if we are to move beyond superficial connections of race, class, and gender. If transformation is truly the goal of any inclusive paradigm, then the lives and experiences of marginalized groups must be placed at the core of the research context (Mertens, 1999). Consequently, the only way to ensure that relevant African perspectives are included in the problem identification/formulation phase is to center the research agenda in the lived experience of African American communities.

An Afrocentric perspective, as it relates to being well-grounded in a people's understanding, involves the researcher's affinity, knowledge, and respect for the history, culture, and knowledge of African-descendant people. This does not preclude non-African group members from conducting culturally competent research; however, the research agenda must serve the interest of the African-descendant persons of study. According to Kershaw (2004), we should ask some or all of the following questions when defining the research question and the antecedents and outcomes concerning a people's life experiences and life chances:

How did they/do they understand relevant historical and contemporary phenomena related to the question?

How have their attitudes and behaviors been shaped and misshaped by this phenomenon?

What are the factors that they see as being important?

How do we know?

Where are their words?

When are they speaking?

Where is their voice?

At the end of the day, the Moynihan Report informed a major presidential address by Lyndon Johnson, unleashed a firestorm of criticism, and began four decades of debate over the connection between Black family life and poverty. The critical reaction to the Moynihan Report resides with the definition, description, and condition of the Black community ushered in by the Black Power Movement. Many critics of the report interpreted this as "blaming the victim." The growing sentiment of racial pride and self-affirmation put researchers on notice that the Black community was no longer going to accept pathological interpretations of its community. This point in social science research was arguably responsible for key changes in social science research, like African-centered, Feminist, and empowerment-based research approaches which will be discussed in the final section of this chapter.

Interpretation

Interpretation is the stage where the researcher translates the results in the context of the purpose of the research.

Where power shows up:

Without input from those being researched, the interpretations of the researchers are vulnerable to internal biases or projections. As we discussed earlier, the concept of an objective reality belongs to a school of thought that believes researchers are objective. Consequently, one can argue that the singular interpretations of a researcher can act as projections that are then used to provide justification for maintaining power and control over their victims. Persons in authority then can blame the powerless for assuming these projections If the powerless fail to assume these projections, those in the more powerful roles can perceive them as having done so anyway or can get angry at them (Bowen, 1978).

In summary, an African proverb says, "Never let the Lion tell the Giraffe's story." This simply means that the Giraffe can never be the hero in a story told by the hunter. The problem begins with the research problem statement and is exacerbated throughout the remaining four stages of the research process. If researchers are trained to always look for a problem they will certainly find one. The voices of the re-searched are absent in the framing of the research questions, the methods used to find the information, and the interpreta-tion of the results. This deficit-based approach to research is exemplified in the Moynihan Report. Is the glass half-empty or half-full? I don't know; let's ask the giraffe.

Democratizing Research

Asa once spoke about an approach that program evaluators and other social scientists really need when engaging in dia-logue with families of African-descended people. When the focus is on African history and culture, rather than deficits and lack of validity, the comments and questions pertain to a sense of belonging, purpose and destiny, and thereby carry forth within the realm of substance and reality. The outcome is much more likely to have true meaning, authenticity and practical orientation. These statements underscore the impor-tance of context in research. Context is social and historical and shapes how one constructs knowledge and understands the surrounding reality. In this final section, I attempt to illus-trate how bias in research can be democratized by using ap-proaches that center the research question in the historical and social context of a person or group. This discussion is designed to show that by using a liberating lens to focus on self-empowerment and opportunity shifts the "problematic" research paradigm to one that is empowering and inherently affirming.

The last 60 years have witnessed a surge in research approaches that are designed to be inclusive, affirming, and empowering for both the researcher and the researched. For that reason, I will limit my discussion to three types of research methods that reflect my own social location as an African American woman trained as a social worker and program

CHAPTER 7: "ARE WE ASKING THE RIGHT QUESTION?"...
By Sarita K. Davis, PhD, MSW

evaluator: African-Centered Research, Feminist Research, and Community-Based Research.

African-Centered Research

Several scholars have made important contributions in defining the concept of African-centered epistemology. Asante (1987) said that an African-centered perspective is an orientation to data that places African people as participants and agents, shaping life chances and experiences. Nobles (1990) says, "The infusion of African and African-American content and intent in the curriculum by definition must be Afrocentric. In terms of curricular content, the education process must (1) refer to the life experiences, history and traditions of African people as the center of analyses; (2) utilize African and African-American liberation and higher-level human functioning; and, (3) assist African-American students in the self-conscious act of creating history" (pp. 20-21). Karenga (1988) makes a similar statement: *"Afrocentricity is essentially a quality of perspective or approach rooted in the cultural image and human interests of African people* [emphasis in the original]" (p. 404). Keto (2001) goes further to argue that any African-centered analysis must begin with Africa.

African-centered scholars generally agree that there is a "centering" of the research in the lived experiences of African people. To be "centered" simply means being well-grounded in the history, culture, and understandings of African people as well possessing its best interests at heart. With the theoretical framework sketched, let us define African-centered Research.

Asante describes a set of basic beliefs that researchers must hold to be considered African-centered (Asante, 1990, 1993, 2008). According to Reviere (2001) these canons, or research criteria, are based on the principles of *MAAT* (meaning, "quest for justice and harmony") and *Nommo* (meaning "productive word"). They are, in Kiswahili: *Ukweli, Utulivu, Uhaki, Ujamaa,* and *Kujitoa.*

> *Ukweli:* The groundedness of research in the experiences of the community being researched.
>
> *Utulivu:* Requires the researcher to actively avoid creating, exaggerating, or sustaining divisions between or within communities and strive for harmony within and between groups.
>
> *Uhaki:* Requires that the researcher ensure that the research process is fair to all participants, especially those being researched.
>
> *Ujamaa:* Requires the researcher to recognize and maintain community and reject the separation between the researcher and participant.
>
> *Kujitoa:* Requires the researcher to make a commitment to the objectives and outcomes of the research.

All elements of the research process from the framing of the research question to the data collection and analysis are closely integrated with the five canons. Researchers are required to pay close attention to the role of power throughout the research process, from the source of the research question to the social and historical contexts of its existence. Critiques of African-Centered Research could argue that this approach does not specifically advocate for a gender-based perspective, which still makes it biased. However, one could use the overarching principle of *MAAT* (justice) as a counterpoint.

Feminist Research

Feminist Research also challenges traditional social science research, in that it acknowledges patriarchal values and beliefs in our social world which shape both the construction and definition of how research is done and how knowledge is determined. Male bias in the world determines how and why research is done and shapes the interpretation of data. The bias is typically that of white, middle-class, heterosexual men (Hawkensworth, 1989). Fundamentally, traditional social science research with its claims to objectivity (in both qualitative and quantitative methods) is flawed because it does not recognize how its own biases impact the research process from the choice of a topic to the final presentation of data.

Methodologically, Feminist Research differs from traditional research in three ways: 1) It actively seeks to remove the power imbalance between research and subject; 2) It is politically motivated and has a major role in changing social inequality; and 3) It begins with the standpoints and experiences of women. Sandra Harding (1987) makes similar claims to the defining features of Feminist Research when she argues that studying women from their perspective, recognizing the researcher as part of the research subject and acknowledging that the beliefs of the researcher shape the research are what distinguish Feminist Research.

Five attributes can characterize a shift toward Feminist Research. First, the unequal relationship between the researcher and the subject is restructured to validate the perspective of the participant. The premise is to remove the hierarchical relationship between researcher and participant. Second, Feminist Research is also defined by its use of feminist concerns and beliefs to ground the research process. Feminism takes women as its starting point, seeking to explore and uncover patriarchal social dynamics and relationships from the perspective of women. Third, Feminist Research is also committed to social change, arising from the actions of women to refuse the patriarchal social structure as it stands in favor of a more egalitarian society. Fourth, Feminist Research addresses the power imbalances between women and men and among women as active agents in the world. Finally, Feminist Research is research that uses feminist principles throughout all stages of research, from choice of topic to presentation of data. These feminist principles also inform and act as the framework guiding the decisions being made by the researcher.

Community-Based Research
Community-Based Research takes place in community settings and involves community members in the design and implementation of research projects. Such activities should demonstrate respect for the contributions of success which are made by community partners as well as respect for the principle of "doing no harm" to the communities involved. In order to achieve these goals, the following principles are used to guide the development of research projects involving collaboration between researchers and community partners, be they community-based organizations or informal groups of individual community members.
Principles:

> Community partners should be involved at the earliest stages of the project, helping to define research objectives and having input into how the project will be organized.
>
> Community partners should have real influence on project direction—that is, enough leverage to ensure that researchers adhere to the project's original goals, mission, and methods.
>
> Research processes and outcomes should benefit the community. Community members should be hired and trained whenever possible and appropriate, and the research should help build and enhance community assets.

Community members should be part of the analysis and interpretation of data and should have input into how the results are distributed. This does not imply censorship of data or of publication, but rather the opportunity to make clear the community's views about the interpretation prior to final publication.

Productive partnerships between researchers and community members should be encouraged to last beyond the life of the project. This will make it more likely that research findings will be incorporated into ongoing community programs and therefore provide the greatest possible benefit to the community from research.

Community members should be empowered to initiate their own research projects that address needs they identify themselves.

Each of the three research approaches discussed here address issues of bias in research from their inception. They acknowledge that history, context, and the active engagement of participants are central in mediating power differentials and producing relevant, useful research.

Conclusion

This essay was not intended to be an exhaustive survey of the multiple ways in which power in research manifests in the social science research process. Rather, it is the author's goal to reiterate Asa's concerns about asking the right question. As stated earlier, my hope is to contribute to the conversation on power and objectivity in research and make oppressive ideologies and methodologies embedded in the social science process more transparent.

To cross over into the land of bias-free research, one has to commit transgressions against epistemological beliefs, leap over disciplinary hurdles, and slay internalized notions of objectivity. While I learned these lessons long ago, it is good to remind myself and others as I continue on my research path. I thank the editors of this book for giving me the opportunity to share my thoughts, knowledge, and experience in the area of bias in research. Sometimes it is good also to remind one another that the struggle is not imaginary—it is quite real.

References

Aponte, H. J. (1994). *Bread & spirit: Therapy with the new poor*. New York: Norton.

Aponte, H. J. (1994). How personal can training get? *Journal of Marital and Family Therapy, 20*, 3–15.

Asante, M. K. (1980). *Afrocentricity*. Trenton, NJ: Africa World Press.

Asante, M. K. (1987). *The Afrocentric idea*. Philadelphia: Temple University Press.

Asante, M. K. (1990). *Kemet, Afrocentricity, and knowledge*. Trenton, NJ: Africa World Press.

Asante, M. K. (1993). *Malcolm X as cultural hero and other Afrocentric essays*. Trenton, NJ: Africa World Press.

Asante, M. K. (2008). *The Afrocentric manifesto*. Cambridge, MA: Polity Press.

Bowen, M. (1978). *Family therapy in clinical practice*. New York: Jason Aronson.

Carruthers, J. (1996). Science and oppression. In Daudi Ajani Ya Azibo (Ed.), *African psychology in historical perspective and related commentary*. Trenton, NJ: Africa World Press.

Collins, P. H. (1991). *Black feminist thought: Knowledge, consciousness, and the politics of empowerment*. Cambridge, MA: Unwin Hyman.

Dixon, V. (1971). African-oriented and Euro-American-oriented worldviews: Research methodologies and economics, *Review of Black Political Economy, (7)*2, 119-156.

Dixon, V. (1976). Worldviews and research methodology. In Lewis King (Ed.), *African philosophy: Assumption and paradigms for research on Black persons*, 51-102. Los Angeles: Fanon R&D Center.

Harding, S. G. (Ed.). (1987). *Feminism and methodology: Social science issues.* Bloomington: Indiana University Press, 1987.

Hawkesworth, M. E. (1989). Knowers, knowing, known: feminist theory and claims of truth. *Signs: Journal of Women in Culture & Society, 14*(3), 533-557.

Hilliard, A. G. (1991). The ideology of intelligence and I.Q. magic in education. In A. G. Hilliard (Ed.), *Testing African American students.* Special re-issue of *The Negro Educational Review, 38*(3), April-July, 1987. Morristown, NJ: Aaron Press.

Hilliard, A. G. (1992). Behavioral style, culture, teaching, and learning. *Journal of Negro Education, (61)*3, 370-377.

Hilliard, A. G. (1995). Either a paradigm shift or no mental measurement: The non-science and nonsense of *the bell curve. Psychological Discourse, 76*(10), 6-20.

Hood, S. (1998). Responsive evaluation Amistad style: Perspectives of one African-American evaluator. In R. Sullivan (Ed.), Proceedings of the Stake Symposium on Educational Evaluation. Urbana-Champaign, IL: University of Illinois at Urbana-Champaign.

Hood, S. (2001). Nobody knows my name: In praise of African American evaluators who were responsive. *New Directions for Evaluation, 92,* 31-43.

Karenga, M. R. (1977). *Kwanzaa: Origin, concepts practice.* Los Angeles: Kawaida.

Karenga, M. R. (1988). Black studies and the problematic of paradigm: The philosophical dimension. *Journal of Black Studies, 18*(4), 395-414.

Kershaw, T. (2003). The Black Studies paradigm: The making of scholar activists. In J. L. Conyers (Ed.), *Afrocentricity and the academy: Essays on theory and practice,* 27-36. Jefferson, NC: McFarland and Company.

Kershaw, T. (2012). Africana Studies and the production of future scholars. *The Western Journal of Black Studies, 34*(2), 292-297.

Keto, C. T. (2001). *Vision and time: historical perspective of an Africa-centered paradigm.* Lanham, MD: University Press of America.

Madison, A.-M. (1992). Primary inclusion of culturally diverse minority program participants in the evaluation process. In A.-M. Madison (Ed.), *Minority Issues in Evaluation.* New directions for program evaluation, no. 53 (35-43). San Francisco: Jossey-Bass.

Mertens, D. (1999). Inclusive evaluation: Implications of transformative theory for evaluation. *American Journal of Evaluation, 20,* 1-14.

Nobles, W. (1985). *Africanity and the Black family: The development of a theoretical model.* Berkeley: Institute for the Advanced Study of Black Family Life and Culture.

Nobles, W. (1989). Psychological Nigrescence: An Afrocentric review. *Counseling Psychologist, 17*(2), 253-57.

Nobles, W. (1990). The infusion of African and African-American content: A question of content and intent. In A. G. Hilliard & L. Payton-Stewart (Eds.), *The infusion of African and African American content in the school curriculum: Proceedings of the first national conference, October 1989.* Morristown, NJ: Aaron Press, 5-24.

Pinderhughes, E. B. (1983). Empowerment for our clients and for ourselves. *Social Casework, 64*(6), 331-338.

Reviere, R. (2001). Toward an Afrocentric research methodology. *Journal of Black Studies, 31*(6), 709-728.

Smith, Linda (2002). *Decolonizing methodologies: Research and indigenous peoples.* London: Zed Books.

NKƆNSƆNKƆNSƆN

(corn-song-corn-song)

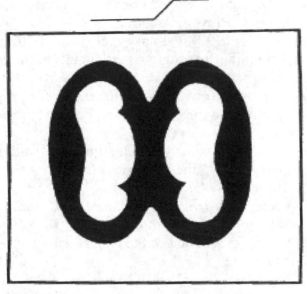

literally :

A CHAIN, or A LINK

Symbol of unity, responsibility, interdependence, brotherhood and cooperation

Saying: *"We are linked in both life and death. Those who share common blood relations never break apart."*

This symbol reflects unity and responsibility. Its meaning relates to the concept of connection with cooperation. It relates human beings to the links of a chain, where the interdependence of each person (link) determines the success of the community (chain).

This is the symbol of human relations.

Chapter 8: Early Socialization and Education

James C. Young, EdD and Ernest D. Washington, PhD

"Africa is the mother of civilization and the land where the very foundations in socialization practices were laid and influenced cultures all over the world. . . . In order to secure our future, we must embrace our past." (Asa G. Hilliard III Nana Baffour Amankwatia II, 2002)

"Our vision is to guarantee the development of the African spirit, mind, and being and the worldwide advancement of African people." (MBONGI Council of Association of Black Psychologists, 1998 conference)

"The education/socialization of any people is a prime responsibility of its members. Any people who abandon this responsibility are certain to disintegrate and lose its potency." (Asa G. Hilliard III Nana Baffour Amankwatia II, 1998)

"There is no chance whatsoever that the masses of our people will be saved unless African people assume primary responsibility for doing so! No one else has our optimal development as their priority! They never have. They never will." (Asa G Hilliard III Nana Baffour Amankwatia II, 1998)

Asa, as he was affectionately known to many throughout the world, was an African who stood tall and taught, spoke, and acted in truth. The statements above from colleagues, friends, and the subject of *Honoring Asa,* set the tone for the final essay in this collection and serve as a clarion call for action. The underlying premise of this essay is the survival of African and African American children and families as members of the African community. We must work hard to ensure a future for our children. If we do not save our own, they will cease to exist and so will our culture. To destroy our children is to destroy ourselves. It is imperative that we embrace our responsibility to save our children. The major obligation for saving our children lies within the African American community. Our gift to the African American community must be our investment in our children. Every generation must answer to the next. What will the next generation say if we leave them at the mercy of the oppressor? We must do as our elders have done. At the conclusion of a program memorializing Asa's father in Bay City, Texas, an elder asked to be heard. Along with others, Asa G. Hilliard II saw the need for children to have a place for schooling. The area was in a low-lying flood plain. The elders got mules, moved lots of dirt and sand, and put the children's school on dry ground. We can do no less. Let us put our children's feet on dry ground.

During its 31st session, in 1976, the United Nations declared 1979 as the International Year of the Child. Countries throughout the world were encouraged to focus attention on the special needs of their children. President Jimmy Carter signed an executive order creating a national Commission for the International Year of the Child. The intent of the commission was to develop a new awareness of the special needs of children growing up in an increasingly complex world. Dr. Hilliard, then Dean of the School of Education at

San Francisco State University, was one of eight scholars invited to participate in writing a series of statements about children. Asa wrote on "Respect[ing] the Child's Culture."

Culture as defined by Nobles (1985) "is a process which gives people a general design for living and patterns for interpreting their reality." He further defines aspects of culture as ideology, ethos, and worldview; its manifestations consist of behavior, values, and attitudes.

An individual's consciousness develops within the context of his or her culture. Marimba Ani (1994) in *Yurugu* tells us that behavior, thought, and institutions are the core products of any culture. Characteristics of a group of people define the group's culture and include religion, language, food, social habits, music, and art. Within this overall framework of cultural attributes we can identify the importance of family life from a child's very beginning.

Hilliard (1976) writes that from the moment of conception, children establish connections—bonding first with mothers. Children learn to speak a complex language from their immediate surroundings. Innately, they are explorers, curious, imitators of behavior, seeking to engage with others. When these aspects of growth and development are viewed from a cultural context, children are not at a disadvantage or deficit in terms of achievement. There is no achievement gap at birth (Delpit, 2012).

To "Do Asa"
When speaking about the African family, Asa Hilliard demonstrated uninhibited enthusiasm. He cared for the family as a unit. At his home going in 2007, Dr. Wade Nobles, one of his closest friends said, "Do Asa." What does this mean? To do Asa is to act on those areas that impact the African family. In an unpublished paper by Dr. Hilliard in November 2001, he outlined a community's obligation to socialize and educate

African children. Why? Strengthening the African family is fundamental to its survival. This is best done through the socialization and education of children.

To "do Asa" is to act on those areas that impact the African family. In an unpublished paper by Dr. Hilliard in November 2001, he outlined a community's obligation to socialize and educate African children. Shown below are the 13 tasks in his outline, requirements that the socialization process must perform to bring about desirable outcomes of being African:

1. Study and know yourself and your people.
2. Model expected behavior.
3. Expose children to the wider world.
4. Involve children in the real world of work, play, joy, pain, and truth.
5. Participate with children in organized groups that serve the interests of the larger community.
6. Give children responsibilities and hold them accountable.
7. Listen well to children's thoughts and feelings.
8. Provide an environment with unconditional respect (not automatic approval).
9. Provide an environment where children are well enough known by significant adults so that they can get mature feedback.
10. Provide an environment for appropriate recognition for children's efforts.
11. Provide an environment where children experience unconditional love.
12. Maintain structures linking elders and youth.
13. Tell and retell the story of one's family and people, so that the children can locate themselves in time, in space, in context, and in destiny.

Countering *Maafa*

The African and African American family continues to suffer from the ravages of history. In her book *Let the Circle Be Unbroken,* Marimba Ani (1980) described *Maafa,* a Kiswahili word that means "disaster," as a system that intentionally enslaved and inhumanly treated Africans. Throughout the disasters caused by the *Maafa,* the African family has been imperiled by one destructive force after another. Perhaps the greatest and longest lasting impact of these destructive acts has happened to children. Instead of experiencing the support and resources that will empower their growth and development—thereby nurturing and energizing their capability as future shapers and progenitors of African culture—our children encounter tidal waves of destructiveness, the opposite of what they need and deserve as human beings. Instead of joining them in the process of Sankofa and the African ideals of *MAAT,* our children are experiencing the terrors of white supremacy, the segregated/apartheid-laden institutions of housing, food distribution, education, school-to-prison pipeline—in short, a socialization and mis-education that denigrates their humanity, squelches their potential, and denies them dignity and respect. As their caretakers and elders we are allowing this handicapping process to occur; we are allowing our children to be socialized and educated outside of their culture.

Any competent professional understands the critical role that culture plays in the growth and development of children. What difference would the socialization and education processes make if these were anchored in a nurturing process derived from an African worldview?

There are at least two perspectives to consider. For African American children to be in environments that are less than nurturing, they often develop negative identities relative

127

to their self-concept and self-image. On the other hand, think about the kind of enrichment experiences the Council for Independent Black Institutions (CIBI) provides for students who attend their schools and gain the benefit of CIBI's social studies curriculum. From their preschool program through the middle grades, CIBI's schools place emphasis on four elements important to the African American community: family, community, nation, and race. Family members are identified as African; members of the community are described as folks who look like them; people from the continent are identified in pictures and books; and race is reinforced by songs, objects, and symbols from Africa.

For further reinforcement, let's look at Africa's unsurpassed natural beauty and history. Some of the noted natural treasures of this great continent are: the Nile River, the Sahara, Mount Kilimanjaro, Lake Victoria, the Congo Basin, Lake Chad, the Great Rift Valley, and so much more. Every country in Africa has its own examples of the natural beauty that permeates the continent. Historical analyses clearly portray Africa as a place where people from other countries traveled and found fully intact cultures. In the Nile Valley alone, we know of established communities whose practices and principles of socialization and education exhibited a long history of success. Recorded history reflects the fact that Europeans had an overwhelming feeling of both admiration and fear of what they saw in African countries. For example, they admired what the Nile Valley cultures had achieved in architecture, education, philosophy, science, mathematics, and more (Hilliard, 2002). Moreover, they also feared what they saw from their worldview and took steps to destroy the physical, architectural, and cultural environment. Their sole mission was to invade, disrupt, steal, and control both the land and the people living there, and this pattern extended beyond the Nile Valley to encompass the entire continent. Such disruption and invasion caused monumental disaster (*Maafa*) to African families. The intent of those disruptions was neither accidental nor benign. The continued destruction of the African American family and the emasculation of the African American male are two ongoing conditions (Nobles, 2006). Forcible entry into countries at peace allowed invaders to wage war and destabilize the family structure. The destabilization enabled invading countries to nearly sever the spiritual, cultural, and family values which permit groups to remain intact, empowering those who invaded the motherland to reign over Africans throughout the Diaspora and across many generations.

Even as we recognize the legitimacy of our descendants' cultural attributes—our connection to *MAAT*—we must acknowledge the damage as well. A close examination of almost any set of statistics on the African American family paints a grim picture. Disproportionately, our families live with extreme stresses. Causes of these stresses are both external and internal and are more acute when there is widespread poverty. External conditions often contribute to factors that cause internal stresses. Some of the major crises that impact our families are: the high percentage of female-headed families; high percentage of unwed African American teenagers giving birth; unemployment/underemployment among youth and adults; rise in child/spousal abuse, crime, drugs, and violence; and disparity in earned income when compared to whites' earned income. Reports on these circumstances abound from the Center for the Study of Social Policy and the Children's Defense Fund, both based in Washington, DC.

In the face of continued opposition and challenging circumstances, we must remember the importance of transmitting African culture to future generations. In the foreword of the book *Know Thy Self* by Dr. Na'im Akbar (1998), Dr. Hilliard wrote about the need for us to see ourselves from a historical perspective and stay connected to our history. Such an understanding will help us to firmly re-establish our spirituality, our family values, and the importance of our cultural foundation. Clarity of our cultural foundation undergirds how we should socialize and educate our children. Ultimately we must change and improve who we are by clarifying and improving our knowledge of African and Diasporan history. Through qualitative socialization and education processes, each generation can transmit to the next those elements which are critical to our survival and our ability to thrive and sustain our future.

Asa Hilliard's writings always addressed the truth of where we as a people stood. His books, including *The Maroon within Us* (1996), *SBA: The Reawakening of the African Mind* (1998), *African Power* (2002), and his many articles always spoke the truth—and spoke truth to power. African power talks about the affirmation of African indigenous socialization. African people are constantly faced with culture wars that usually involve Europeans' efforts to compel everyone else to practice their values, traditions, religions, beliefs, and lifestyles. Socialization and education are essential to the well-being of the African and African American family. Oppressors live in fear of the one variable that we lack—unity as a people. As Asa understood and urged us to work toward, African-centered socialization and education processes would be the hallmark of unity, toward which our people must strive and collectively achieve.

This process must begin among our children. The mission of early socialization is critical to the future of the African family. Our mission must begin with the understanding that African people laid the foundation for education and socialization. This essay will examine some of the early principles and practices of education and socialization and the value of returning to these early principles and practices relative to the future of our children and families. We must know who we were before we came to this time and place so that we can reposition ourselves and our culture educationally, economically, and socially.

Background: Education and Socialization

The future of any people is entirely dependent on the socialization of its children (Rashid, 1984). Through socialization, children acquire their culture's norms, values, and belief patterns, forming the basis for how they will live throughout their lives. From this foundation each generation passes on to the next those elements that will sustain them. The quality of life evolves from a cultural foundation. As with any culture, intergenerational transmission is a major factor in the status of the African American community. Why? The transmission of culture is generally done within the context of the family. Central to the socialization process are parents. During childhood, mothers are primarily the focal parent. It is she who plants the foundation of values, behaviors, character, and beliefs. While fathers have a vital role in terms of transmitting values, beliefs, and other fundamental elements of growth and development, fathers' absence due to underemployment/ unemployment, domestic relations with the mother, incarceration, and other difficulties can place the responsibilities of children's upbringing on the mother, her family members, and the surrounding community.

We must locate where we are. African/African American families are in a crisis. The magnitude of the situation is such that the community has to make a decisive change. That change must lead to recovery, or death may be inevitable.

Still, Dr. Hilliard always painted a picture of hope for the disenfranchised. In "doing Asa" we must channel our thoughts and activities in that direction as well.

The two processes that impact children's development and future are those of socialization and education. Consider process as a way, a method, or a plan with some end in mind. The end in this case is children—their growth, their well-being, and their identity as African-descended people. Clarity on who we are and where we stand will serve as an underpinning of where we go in the future. Akbar (1985, 1994) tells us:

> To cultivate that community consciousness in the child, he shouldbe viewed as a community offspring, rather than just an offspring of his biological parents. . . . The child, in turn, learns to see himself as secure in the community and responsible to all members of that community. . . . Another vehicle for maintaining a broadened scope in the child's education is the study of world religions, their origins and consistencies. In such a way, the child will view religion as a worldwide phenomena and not just in the limited sense of somebody's invention. He will understand religion as a body of knowledge geared toward guiding the complete development of man. . . . Such knowledge lays the foundation for proper human development." (*The Community of Self,* revised edition, pp. 70, 77)

Therefore, we can say that socialization is a way, a method, a plan that centers us within ourselves and extends outward amongst one another as we bond with our people, our history, and our Creator.

CHAPTER 8: EARLY SOCIALIZATION AND EDUCATION
By James C. Young, EdD and Ernest D. Washington, PhD

Education is a method of sharing or obtaining knowledge, particularly directed at empowering our ability to discern and otherwise apply what we understand. All groups of people use what we call education as a vehicle to transmit knowledge to advance and sustain its community. "Educate" means to bring out from within someone, to draw out the potential. Amos Wilson (1991) tells us that Black children have great, great potential. As a community we are reminded in Asa's *SBA: The Reawakening of the African Mind* (1998) of the transformative purpose and process of teaching. He tells us of the three keys necessary to bring out the best in our children through the processes of socialization and education: Preparation, consciousness, and willingness are the ingredients necessary to develop the genius in African children.

As we have noted, early socialization and early education are fundamental. In the case of our children today, which path are we preparing children to follow—life or death? In James Baldwin's *The Evidence of Things Not Seen* (1985), he said that children have blind trust in adults, but when adults fail them, children lose all confidence and run to their death. Death may take different forms, different paths, and different rates of occurrence; however we perceive of it nowadays, the crisis among families and children resembles death more than life.

Asa Hilliard (1991) and Amos Wilson (1991) have said that our children possess genius; what we have to do is to unlock it. The degree of destructiveness and the loss of so many lives due to mis-education, incarceration, domestic violence, health-related factors and other crisis-level events requires urgency and strong, genius-equivalent responsiveness. We must gather methods, ways, and plans that embrace our own and children's innate genius, or face the eventual path of death for our community. Life or death—you may wonder how such contrasting paths can be redirected. Like Asa said, preparation, consciousness, and will are a lot to ask of our community. Can we do this on behalf of our children and our future as a culture? Are we prepared to do this? Do we possess the level of consciousness needed to do this? Are we willing? How one is socialized and educated can often be the contributing factor in life's choices. What are the choices facing us? How will the choices affect future generations? What role will elders play? It is important to examine the landscape of the African American family.

Educating the Black Child

Where Do We Stand?

If we do not save our own, they will cease to exist. It is imperative that we embrace our responsibility to save our children: The major obligation for saving our own lies within the African American community.

In the late 1990s, the late Dr. Asa Hilliard convened a four-day think tank with a number of noted scholars from throughout the Diaspora. At the conclusion of the meeting, the group centered their collective thoughts on the following statements: "There is no chance whatsoever that the masses of our people will be saved unless African people assume primary responsibility for doing so! No one else has our optimal development as their highest priority. They never have. They never will."

Before his untimely departure in 2007, an informal conversation with Asa concluded with us saying that unless things change, dramatically, many of our children were doomed. Still, it was extremely difficult to use the "D" word: DOOMED. If you knew Asa, you knew he would not say anything of that magnitude without doing his homework.

Do your homework was his war cry in the battle to prevent any more young people from heading prematurely toward death—while also developing methods and plans for them to march confidently along life's pathways instead.

What Are the Challenges?

In *SBA,* Dr. Hilliard tells us that we must reawaken the African mind and do so for a specific purpose—teaching ourselves and one another. He was inclusive about identifying present and potential African teachers, noting that wise elders were among those with formal academic certification and those working in barbershops, after-school programs and recreational centers. The point to keep in mind was that all of us who call ourselves African teachers or are *de facto* African teachers are critical to the future of African people. It behooves us to make sure we are prepared, conscious, and willing as we go about the endeavor of teaching in numerous ways and various settings. However, whenever and wherever we do this, we must prepare ourselves—this is extremely important.

More recently at a faculty meeting (January, 2012), in the School of Education at Clark Atlanta University, a senior administrator from the Southern Region Education Board, an Atlanta-based education corporation, reported that in its infancy the organization wanted to improve the quality of education in the southern states. Startlingly, he reported that in 1948 the high school graduation rate of African American males was roughly 40%. When you juxtapose the average high school graduation rates of African American males in 2010, 47%, you see that not much has changed in 62 years (Jackson & Holzman, 2010). Among the many reports that we have studied recently, one indicated that without a high school education more than 60% of our males will be incarcerated (Western & Pettit, 2010). We can consider this as taking a low dose of poison every day—drug use, no schooling, crime, violence, and the like. Eventually, the mind of a person with this lifestyle will become paralyzed for lack of use or misuse and it will be unusable. We must remember that the mind and body can only sustain so much damage. How much longer can we stand by and watch this cataclysmic action before we act? Are we too late? Have we created a "new slave"—men in prison—for the oppressors' system?

How do we stop the bleeding? When is enough enough? When will the African American community decide we can't take it anymore? When will we stop the bleeding? Have we become insensitive to the conditions of our children, youth, and families?

What Is the Hope for the Future?
How we as Africans and African Americans socialize and educate our children will determine how we as a people will survive and thrive. We must have a vision that will provide the highest possible education for them. The education of our children is an urgent necessity. We cannot abide another generation of children whose socialization we have neglected. We can no longer permit them to invent their own systems. We have left them without the direction of a community of conscious teachers and elders. This is unacceptable and must change because we change it—we must embrace our role as our children's caretakers, guides, and elders.

In his wisdom, Asa (1982) taught us that education and socialization processes must minimally teach our children:
1. **Reality** – Teach them about the world as it really is, not as others want us to believe it is.
2. **Identity** – The past two generations are confused about who they are. There is less of a sense of be longing to one's people and ethnic family.

3. **Purpose** – School programs and "education reform" language do not help young people to develop a purpose in life.
4. **Information** – Young people need to be exposed to information and experiences that pertain to the richness of African people.
5. **Responsibility** – We must teach our children to make decisions, act on them, and understand the nature of consequences. How one is socialized impacts his or her future.

Do we know what time it is? Are we willing to do better than we have for the past few decades? What will the future hold for our children—requiem or resurrection? In the closing scenes of Spike Lee's film *School Daze* (1988), Laurence Fishburne's character Vaughn Dunlap pleaded with us to wake up. As a community do we have the will to wake up? There are consequences for not waking up. If we are to heed the urgent words of elders like Asa Hilliard, we must will ourselves to take on the responsibility of reawakening the minds of our children.

If the future is going to be substantially different for the next generation, we must 1) look at the problems and situations from a new and different viewpoint; 2) develop new ways, methods, and plans for the coming age; and 3) act with preparation, consciousness, willingness, and urgency.

> Our deepest fear is not that we are inadequate. Our deepest fear is that we are powerful beyond measure. It is our light, not our darkness that most frightens us. We ask ourselves, Who am I to be brilliant, gorgeous, talented, and fabulous? Actually,

who are you *not* to be? You are a child of
God. Your playing small does not serve the
world. There is nothing enlightened about
shrinking so that other people won't feel
insecure around you. . . . We were born to
manifest the glory of God that is within
us. It's not just in some of us; it's in everyone. And as we let our own light shine, we
unconsciously give other people permis-
sion to do the same. As we are liberated
from our fears, our presence automatically
liberates others. (Williamson, 1992, pp.
190-191)

To Be African is a collection of essays by Africans
edited by Gallman, Ani, & Williams (2003). The essays capture what we believe is the essence of being an African. From
these essays, we derived a set of statements to guide us as we
consider what is at stake about our survival and what is hope-
ful:

- **To be African** (Asa G. Hilliard III) is to answer the
  question "To be African or not to be?" African people
  have undergone a systematic assault on them for more
  than four centuries, which continues in different forms
  today. Think of the bear in the arcade; he is constantly
  being shot at. Each shot turns him in another direction. The bear becomes disoriented. Eventually, the
  bear falls over but gets up, attempting to find a sense
  of direction. In our own continuous onslaught, we have
  had to call on our reserves in order to stay alive. To
  be African is to point ourselves in a direction that will
  make us victorious. As a people we have been disoriented about what we must do and the fuzziness must
  end so we can be clear. The decision to be African

brings each of us into the global African community. Such a decision connects us to a history and culture that transcend the oppressors' physical and mental treat ment of us. Such a decision connects us to our ancestors and challenges us to kindle a revolutionary act of liberation. In the words of Wade Nobles (1970; Williams, 2008), "I am because we are, and because we are therefore I am." To be African is the solution.

- **To be African** (Marimba Ani) means that we are bonded by a culture of origin. We share a common culture that ties us to values, customs, traditions, and a shared heritage. Through a shared culture we have collective identity. Through cultural continuity, a people can connect with their historical past.

- **To be African** (Wade Nobles) is to recognize that no matter what documents are produced, critically acclaimed or not, we cannot be disconnected from our rich past. Every effort to physically punish us, psychologically shame us, and sociologically disorient us has not torn us asunder. To be made to feel less than human was part of an ongoing plan to "de-Africanize" Black people. Nobles tells us that we must re-focus our efforts and gain control over whatever it takes to heal us as a people.

- **To be an African elder** (Baba Hannibal Afrik) is to face daily challenges regarding our self-determination. The connecting element for us is our culture. It ties us to our roots, native land, and heritage. Without that connection we will fall into an abyss. As we navigate the daily struggles of life, it is important that we do so through our cultural lens. The cultural lens enables us to maintain our sense of dignity and self-worth. A cultural lens permits us to see things that are parallel or congruent in our history and things that flow from our Ancestors to us and beyond. One of the stabilizing forces in our existence is our consciousness. A collective consciousness is a dimension of the African community. It is transmitted by the elders in the community. Elders serve as role models; they are given respect for their service in the community and provide leadership to the youth and young adults. Baba Afrik tells us that programs such as "rites of passage" represent a correct step that will help us to regain self-respect and reclaim our families. "Rites of passage" programs will help to restore the socialization process of our children and youth.

- **To be an African teacher** (Asa G. Hilliard III) is to know that African people have a long recorded history of deep thought and educational excellence. Teaching and shaping character is one of our great strengths. Therefore, tapping the genius in our children should not surprise any of us. When it comes to socializing and educating our children, we must focus intensively on two primary reasons:

1. We have the best developed teaching and socialization practices ever established anywhere in the world;
2. The primary tool of our oppression is miseducation by our oppressors. The African community must gain control over the education and socialization of African children.

African teachers have high character and deep regard and respect for our Ancestors. These teachers do not accept minimal standards as benchmarks for excellence within themselves or among the children they teach. Therefore, these teachers maintain high levels of preparation and insist on the same among the children. African teachers are of high moral quality and do what is necessary to bring out the genius in our children. Generally, they have what it takes to be enormously successful in the classroom. They have the will to do for children those things that ignite everyone's thinking processes.

- **To be an African professional** (Esmeralda Simmons, Esq.) is to apply the meaning described in a parable of when Africa was green, fertile, and flourishing several hundred years ago. Then the *Maafa* happened. Numerous catastrophes occurred in the homeland. The lands went dry; people were thirsty and weak. Water became the utmost element for survival. The African people knew of a large watering hole very far away. It was controlled by the oppressors. An oasis of major proportions developed around the watering hole. Africans had no access, but they strategized how they would get water. They trained a small group of very intelligent boys and girls to become experts on moving volumes of water. Africans knew the enemy would trade water for other goods. The mission of the youth was to study how to move the water. It was an expensive and long-term proposition, but over time it would impact the quality of life for the Africans. Therefore, they spared no expense to carry out the mission. Living at the oasis was quite different for the chosen youth. They became accustomed to a standard they had not experienced back in the village; there was good quality housing, plenty of food and entertainment, a large assortment of clothes and other luxuries. The mission became secondary. As the years passed, the students became very knowledgeable about methology in moving water from one area to another.

They also acquired a lot of worldly ways that they learned from the culture imposed within the oasis.

Eventually a messenger came from their village to see the progress the youth had made. The messenger easily saw that they had developed gluttonous behaviors and were not eager to return home. After much squabbling, the messenger decided to leave. A few of the youth called out that they would seek help from an agency that had well-trained people who were prepared, conscious about the village's purpose for sending the youth, and willing to assist in the youth's developing genius and growing cultural awareness.

The moral of the story is to not forget the original purpose of the training. As trained professionals, Africans cannot afford to lose sight of why we were trained. Africans and African-descended people must remember to be of service to the community for liberation and self-determination.

- **To Be an African Home Shule** (Mwalimu A. Bomani Baruti and Yaa Mawusi Baruti) is to open one's home to African children. It means to create a safe haven for our children: Provide an alternative education and socialization to public schools which give a mis-education and therefore prevent children from having the means of surviving and thriving in the new world economy. When we decide to host an African Shule in our home we accept the responsibility of providing a direct connection between the past and the present which paves a firm path toward the future in our children's African minds.

- **To Be African** is to embrace many other important facets; to know, for example, the value of being an African Revolutionary, an African Artist, an African Father, and an African Teenager.

CHAPTER 8: EARLY SOCIALIZATION AND EDUCATION
By James C. Young, EdD and Ernest D. Washington, PhD

Kambon (1992) reminds us that we exist in a world dominated by Eurocentric supremacy and racial discrimination. When the slave ships came through the Middle Passage, they brought with them millions of Africans. Brutality and denigration was the order of the day for nearly 300 years. This torture did not strip our Ancestors of who they were. They were forced to take on a pseudo-persona for survival. Several centuries of imprinting have incurred lasting psychological effects. The challenge is to lose the psychological shackles; we can then have a freeing of the mind and return to the "source" as Asa Hilliard described in *Free Your Mind* (1986) and elsewhere. The continued challenges of African people in the motherland and in North America, South America, and the Caribbean revolve around psychological liberation. We must free our minds. We must counter the *Maafa* by adhering to, understanding, and living up to the principles of *MAAT*—truth, justice, order, righteousness, balance, reciprocity, and harmony. In these principles and practices lives the hope for our future.

References

Akbar, N. (1985, 1994). *The community of self* (revised edition). Tallahassee, FL: Mind Productions & Associates.

Akbar, N. (1998). *Know thy self.* Tallahassee, FL: Mind Productions & Associates.

Akoto, A., & CIBI (Eds.). (1990). *Positive African images for children.* Trenton, NJ: Red Sea Press.

Ani, M. (1980). *Let the circle be unbroken.* New York: Nkonimfo Publications.

Ani, M. (1994). *Yurugu: An African-centered critique of European culture, thought, and behavior.* Trenton, NJ: African World Press.

Baldwin, J. (1985). *The evidence of things not seen.* New York: Holt, Rinehart and Winston.

Delpit, L. (2012). *"Multiplication is for white people." Raising expectations for other people's children.* New York: New Press.

Gallman, B., Ani, M., & Williams, L. (2003). *To be Afrikan: Essays by Africans in the process of Sankofa: Returning to the source.* Atlanta: MAAT.

Hilliard, A. G. (1979). *Respect the child's culture.* Atlanta: Author.

Hilliard, A. G. (1982). *Strengths: African-American children and families.* New York: Workshop Center for Open Education, City College.

Hilliard, A. G. (1986). *Free your mind: Return to the source.* VHS videotape. Columbia, SC: Wa'set Educational Productions.

Hilliard, A. G. (1994). *Homework.* Unpublished paper, presented at annual meeting of National Alliance of Black School Educators. Los Angeles.

Hilliard, A. G. (1995). *The Maroon within us: Selected essays on African American community socialization.* Baltimore: Black Classic Press.

Hilliard, A. G. (1997). *Free your mind: Return to the source.* Atlanta: Author.

Hilliard, A. G. (1997). *SBA: The reawakening of the African mind.* Gainesville, FL: Makare Publishing.

Hilliard, A. G. (2001). *Tapping the genius and touching the spirit: A human approach to the rescue of our children. The ninth annual Benjamin E. Mays lecture.* Atlanta: Georgia State University.

Hilliard, A. G. (2001). *Socialization and education: A community obligation.* Unpublished paper.

Hilliard, A. G. (2002). *African power: Affirming African indigenous socialization in the face of the culture wars.* Gainesville, FL: Makare Publishing.

Hilliard, A. G., & Payton-Stewart, L. (1990). *The infusion of African and African-American content in the school curriculum.* Chicago: Third World Press.

Jackson, J., & Holzman, M. (2010). *Yes we can, the Schott 50 state report on public education and Black males.* Cambridge, MA: Schott Foundation for Public Education. Retrieved from http://www.schott foundation. org/publications/schott-2010-black-male-report.pdf

Kambon, K. (1992). *The African personality in America: An African-centered framework.* Tallahassee, FL: Nubian National Publications.

Nobles, W. W. (1985). *Africanity and the Black family: The development of a theoretical model.* Oakland: Institute for the Advanced Study of Black Family Life and Culture.

Nobles, W. W. (1986). *African psychology: Toward its reclamation, reascension & revitalization.* Oakland: Institute for the Advanced Study of Black Family Life and Culture.

Nobles, W. W. (April, 1989). Psychological Nigrescence: An Afrocentric review. *Counseling Psychologist, 17*(2), 253-257.

Nobles, W. W. (2006). *Seeking the Sakhi: Foundational writings for an African psychology.* Chicago: Third World Press.

Rashid, H. (1984). The political socialization of African-American children and youth: The key to future political empowerment. *Journal of Social and Behavioral Sciences, 30,* 28-30.

Western, B., Pettit, B., Economic Mobility Project, & Public Safety Performance Project. (2010). Collateral costs: Incarceration's effect on economic mobility. Washington, DC: The Pew Charitable Trusts. Retrieved from ww.pewtrusts.org/uploadedFiles/wwwpew trustsorg/ Reports/Economic_Mobility/Collateral Costs FINAL.pdf

Williams, R. L. (August, 2008). A 40-year history of the Association of Black Psychologists (ABPsi). *Journal of Black Psychology, 34*(3), 249-260.

Williamson, M. (1992). *A return to love: Reflections on the principles of a course in miracles.* New York: HarperCollins.

Wilson, A. (1991). *Awakening the natural genius of Black children.* Bronx, NY: Afrikan World Infosystems.

Chapter 9: Selected Papers and Articles by Dr. Asa Hilliard

Dr. Asa Hilliard wrote countless papers and spoke widely at national and international organizations. They are to numerous to list here. This selected list is to provide readers with a flavor of his books, journal articles and speeches.

Hilliard, Asa G. (1978) "The Egyptian Mystery System, Greek Philosophy and Dr. George G.M. James." Uraeus 1, No. 2, 46-48.

Hilliard, Asa G. (1978) Free Your Mind, Return to the Source: The African Origins of Civilization. San Francisco: Urban Institute for Human Services.

Hilliard, Asa G. (1982) "Basic Family Bibliography on African and African American History and Culture. Return to the Source 1, No. 4, 13.

Hilliard, Asa G. (1984) Kemetic Concepts in Education. Nile Valley Civilizations: Proceedings of the Nile Valley Conference, Atlanta, September 26-30. Edited by Ivan Van Sertima. New Brunswick Journal of African Civilization, 153-62.

Hilliard, Asa G. (1985) Afterword to the Wonderful Ethiopians of the Ancient Cushite Empire. By Drucilla Dunjee Houston, Baltimore, MD, Black Classic Press.

Hilliard, Asa G. (1985) Blacks in Antiquity: A Review. African Presence in Early Europe. Edited by Ivan Van Sertima. New Brunswick, NJ. Journal of African Civilizations, 90-95.

Hilliard, Asa G. (1985) Introduction to Stolen Legacy, by George G.M. James. San Francisco, CA. Julian Richardson Associates.

Hilliard, Asa G. (1986) Foreword to Golden Names for a Golden People: African and Arabic Names, by Nia Damali. Atlanta Blackwood Press.

Hilliard, Asa G. (1986) "Pedagogy in Ancient Kemet." Kemet and the African Worldview: Research, Rescue and Restoration. Edited by Maulana Karenga and Jacob H. Carruthers. Los Angeles, CA. University of Sankore Press, 131-50.

Hilliard, Asa G. (1986) The Cultural Unity of Black Africa: The Domains of Patriarchy and of Matriarchy in Classic Antiquity." Great African Thinkers, Vol 1, Cheikh Anta Diop. Edited by Ivan Van Sertima and Larry Obadele Williams. New Brunswick, NJ. Journal of African Civilization, 102-109.

Hillard, Asa G. (1989) Introduction to From the Browder File, by Anthony T. Browder. Washington, D.C.: Institute of Karmic Guidance.

Hilliard, Asa G. (1989) Kemetic (Egyptian) Historical Revision: Implications for Cross Cultural Evaluation and Research in Education." Evaluation Practice 10, No 2, 7-23.

Hilliard, Asa G. (1989) "Waset, The eye of Ra and the Abode of Maat: The Pinnacle of Black Leadership in the Ancient world." Egypt Revisited. Rev. ed. Edited by Ivan Van Sertima. New Brunswick, NJ. Journal of African Civilizations, 211-38.

Hilliard, Asa G. (1990) "Ancient Africa's Contribution to Science and Technology." NSBE National Society of Black engineers Magazine 1, No 2, 72-75.

Hilliard, Asa G. (1991) Foreword to Kemet and Other Ancient African Civilizations: Selected References, compiled by Vivian Verdell Gordon. Chicago, IL. Third World Press.

CHAPTER 9: SELECTED PAPERS AND ARTICLES
By Dr. Asa Hilliard

Hilliard, Asa G. (1991) A Selected Bibliography and Outline on African-American History from Ancient Times to the Present: A Resource Packet. Rev. ed. Atlanta.

Hilliard, Asa G. (1992) The Meaning of KMT (Ancient Egyptian) History for Contemporary African-American Experience." Phylon 49, Nos. 1-2, 10-22.

Hilliard, Asa G. (1994) The Maroon Within Us. Baltimore Black Press.

Hilliard, Asa G. (1994) HOMEWORK – Presented to the National Alliance of Black School Educators, Annual meeting, Los Angeles, CA.

Hilliard, Asa G. (1995) Testing African American Students (Ed). Third World Press, Chicago, IL.

Hilliard, Asa G. (1997) SBA: The Reawakening of the African Mind: Foreword by Wade W. Nobles, Gainesville, Fl. Makare Publishing Company.

Hilliard, Asa G. (1998) Foreword to Know Thy Self, by Na'im Akbar. Mind Productions & Associates, Tallahassee, FL.

Hilliard, Asa G. (2000) The State of African Education.n Presented at American Educational Research Association, New Orleans, LA.

Hilliard, Asa G. (2002) A Response to the National Research Council Report: Minority Students in Special and Gifted Education. Council for Exceptional Children Annual Meeting, New York.

Hilliard, Asa G. (2002) African Power Affirming Indigenous Socialization in the Face of the Culture Wars. Gainesville, FL. Makare Publishing Company.

Hilliard, Asa G. (2003) True of Voice: Poetry of Listervelt Middleton.

NSAA
(n-sah)

NEA ONNIM NSAA OTO N'AGO

literally :

HE WHO DOES NOT KNOW THE REAL DESIGN WILL TURN TO AN IMITATION
i.e., HE WHO DOES NOT KNOW AUTHENTIC NSAA WILL BUY THE FAKES

Symbol of excellence, genuineness and authenticity

It refers to the genuineness and authenticity of an object. It reflects excellence and is intended to discourage satisfaction with objects of lower quality or of second nature.

Nsaa is also a symbol of the court historians.

Chapter 10: Contributors

James C. Young, Ed.D. Is professor of early childhood education and Chair of the Department of Curriculum and Instruction at Clark Atlanta University? He is a graduate of Winston-Salem State University, Indiana State University, and the University of Massachusetts, where he obtained his Ed.D. in early childhood education, with a cognate in school administration. Dimensions: The Journal of Early Childhood Education 25 (4): 82, named Dr. Young as one of the top early childhood education scholars in the 20th century. His books include Demythologizing Inner City Children (Co-ed, 1976), From Roots to Wings: Successful Parenting African American Style (2006). He also writes in the areas of child development, play, and teaching and learning. He is also a founding member of ISAAC- Institute for the Study of African American Children, Wayne State University.

Dr. Itihari Y. Toure has worked in the field of education, the Black church, and with Black Women since 1975. Itihari Toure, an ordained elder in the Presbyterian church, currently serves as the Christian education director for the Center for African Biblical Studies (CFABS) and Director of the Sankofa Center for Quality Enhancement and Data Evaluation at the Interdenominational Theological Center (ITC) where she previously worked as program administrator and grants writer in the Office of Black Women in Church and Society (BWCS) since 1993. She teaches as an adjunct professor in the Masters in Christian Education at the ITC. Itihari is one of the conveners for The Jegna Collective. She has also served as a curriculum specialist and college professor at Loyola Marymount University in Los Angeles, Morris Brown College, Reinhardt College, Clark Atlanta University and Georgia State University. Her educational pursuits of degrees to obtain a B.A. in Education and Psychology, a M.A. in Human Development and a Doctorate in Educational Leadership was all under girded by her study with and mentoring by Dr. Asa G. Hilliard III, noted psychologist and educator.

Chike Akua is an educator with several years experience teaching in the Virginia and Georgia public school systems. In 1995 he was named "Teacher of the Year" by the Newport, VA public schools. His books include Reading Revolution (2001), A Treasure within Stories of Remembrance and Rediscovery (2001), and words of Power (2005). He holds a BA in education from Hampton University and an MA in education from Clark Atlanta University. Chike is currently a Ph.D. candidate at Georgia State University. He lectures extensively on teaching and promoting children's interest in learning.

Charlyn Harper Browne, Ph.D. is Senior Associate, Center for the Study of Social Policy, Washington, D.C. She manages the Quality Improvement Center on Early Childhood (QIC –EC), a five-year project of the federal Administration for Children and Families, the Children's Bureau, the National Center for Infants, Toddlers and Families and the Alliance of Children's Trust and Prevention Funds that is coordinated by CSSP. She holds Ph.D. from Georgia State University in Early Childhood Education, an MA in Educational Psychology from Atlanta University and a BA from Spelman College.

Sarita K. Davis, Ph.D., MSW is associate professor, School of Social Work, Georgia State University, Atlanta. She has been published or has advised graduate students' writing on numerous occasions, including the Journal of Black Studies (2009, 2010, and 2013) and the Journal of Multi-Disciplinary Evaluation (2010). She received her MSW from University of

California Los Angeles and her Ph.D. from Cornell University. Her research interests include: HIV/AIDS, student learning, and community-based program evaluation.

Reverend Dr. Mark A. Lomax is founding pastor of First African Presbyterian Church in Lithonia, Georgia, and has served there since 1993. Since 1998 he has been assistant professor of homiletics at the Interdenominational Theological Center (ITC) in Atlanta. His published writings include Jesus and the Hip-hop Generation (co-author Stephany Jackson, 2005); his profile of Marcus Garvey appears in Makers of Christian Theology in America (1997). He received a BA from Heidelberg University, an MDivinity from Trinity Lutheran Seminary, and a DMinistry from United Theological Seminary.

Ernest D. Washington, Ph.D. is a professor in the Department of Teacher Evaluation and Curriculum Studies, University of Massachusetts, Amherst. He obtained his BA degrees from Southern Illinois University and the University of Minnesota, and obtained an MA and Ph.D. from the University of Illinois. His courses at the University of Massachusetts are among those in the master's degree concentration of child study and early education. His professional interests include early childhood education, educational psychology, group counseling, multicultural counseling, and diversity and change.